Microsoft®

MOS 2010 Study Guide for Microsoft® OneNote

John Pierce

PUBLISHED BY
Microsoft Press
A Division of Microsoft Corporation
One Microsoft Way
Redmond, Washington 98052-6399

Library of Congress Control Number: 2011942373
ISBN: 978-0-7356-6594-1

Microsoft Press books are available through booksellers and distributors worldwide. If you need support related to this book, email Microsoft Press Book Support at mspinput@microsoft.com. Please tell us what you think of this book at http://www.microsoft.com/learning/booksurvey.

Acquisitions Editor: Rosemary Caperton
Technical Reviewer: Todd Meister
Copy Editor: Roger LeBlanc
Indexer: Audrey Marr
Editorial Production: Waypoint Press
Cover: Jelvetica

Contents

Taking a Microsoft Office Specialist Exam

Desktop computing proficiency is increasingly important in today's business world. As a result, when screening, hiring, and training employees, employers can feel reassured by relying on the objectivity and consistency of technology certification to ensure the competence of their workforce. As an employee or job seeker, you can use technology certification to prove that you already have the skills you need to succeed, saving current and future employers the trouble and expense of training you.

Microsoft Office Specialist Certification

Microsoft Office Specialist certification for Microsoft Office 2010 is designed to assist employees in validating their skills with programs in the Office 2010 software suite. The following certification paths are available:

- A Microsoft Office Specialist (MOS) is an individual who has demonstrated proficiency by passing a certification exam in one or more of the Office 2010 programs, including Microsoft Word, Excel, PowerPoint, Outlook, OneNote, and Access, or in Microsoft SharePoint.
- A Microsoft Office Specialist Expert (MOS Expert) is an individual who has taken his or her knowledge of Office 2010 to the next level and has demonstrated by passing a certification exam that he or she has mastered the more advanced features of Word 2010 or Excel 2010.

Selecting a Certification Path

When deciding which certifications you would like to pursue, you should assess the following:

- The program and program version(s) with which you are familiar
- The length of time you have used the program and how frequently you use it
- Whether you have had formal or informal training in the use of that program
- Whether you use most or all of the available program features

- Whether you are considered a go-to resource by business associates, friends, and family members who have difficulty with the program

Candidates for MOS-level certification are expected to successfully complete a wide range of standard business tasks, such as formatting a document or worksheet and its content; creating and formatting visual content; locating information in a notebook; or working with SharePoint lists, libraries, Web Parts, and dashboards. Successful candidates generally have six or more months of experience with the specific Office program, including either formal, instructor-led training or self-study using MOS-approved books, guides, or interactive computer-based materials.

Candidates for MOS Expert-level certification are expected to successfully complete more complex tasks that involve using the advanced functionality of the program. Successful candidates generally have at least six months, and may have several years, of experience with the programs, including formal, instructor-led training or self-study using MOS-approved materials.

Test-Taking Tips

Every MOS certification exam is developed from a set of exam skill standards (referred to as the objective domain) that are derived from studies of how the Office 2010 programs or SharePoint are used in the workplace. Because these skill standards dictate the scope of each exam, they provide critical information about how to prepare for certification. This book follows the structure of the published exam objectives; see "Using This Book to Study for a Certification Exam" later in this section for more information.

The MOS certification exams for the Office 2010 programs and SharePoint are performance based and require you to complete business-related tasks in the program for which you are seeking certification. You might be told to adjust program settings or be presented with a file and told to do something specific with it. Your score on the exam reflects how well you perform the requested tasks within the allotted time.

Here is some helpful information about taking the exam:

- Keep track of the time. You have 50 minutes to complete the exam. Your exam time does not officially begin until after you finish reading the instructions provided at the beginning of the exam. During the exam, the amount of time remaining is shown at the bottom of the exam interface. You can't pause the exam after you start it.
- Pace yourself. At the beginning of the exam, you will be told how many questions are included in the exam. Some questions will require that you complete more than

one task. During the exam, the number of completed and remaining questions is shown at the bottom of the exam interface.

- Read the exam instructions carefully before beginning. Follow all the instructions provided in each question completely and accurately.
- Enter requested information as it appears in the instructions, but without duplicating the formatting unless you are specifically instructed to do so. For example, the text and values you are asked to enter might appear in the instructions in bold and underlined text, but you should enter the information without applying these formats.
- Close all dialog boxes before proceeding to the next exam question unless you are specifically instructed not to do so.
- Don't close task panes before proceeding to the next exam question unless you are specifically instructed to do so.
- If you are asked to print a document, worksheet, chart, notebook page, report, or slide, perform the task, but be aware that nothing will actually be printed.
- Don't worry about extra keystrokes or mouse clicks. Your work is scored based on its result, not on the method you use to achieve that result (unless a specific method is indicated in the instructions).
- If a computer problem occurs during the exam (for example, if the exam does not respond or the mouse no longer functions) or if a power outage occurs, contact a testing center administrator immediately. The administrator will restart the computer and return the exam to the point where the interruption occurred, with your score intact.

Certification Benefits

At the conclusion of the exam, you will receive a score report, indicating whether you passed the exam. You can print with the assistance of the testing center administrator. If your score meets or exceeds the passing standard (the minimum required score), you will be contacted by email by the Microsoft Certification Program team. The email message you receive will include your Microsoft Certification ID and links to online resources, including the Microsoft Certified Professional site. On this site, you can download or order a printed certificate, create a virtual business card, order an ID card, view and share your certification transcript, access the Logo Builder, and access other useful and interesting resources, including special offers from Microsoft and affiliated companies.

Using the Logo Builder, you can create a personalized certification logo that includes the MOS logo and the specific programs in which you have achieved certification. If you achieve MOS certification in multiple programs, you can include up to six of them in one logo.

Microsoft Access 2010 Certified
Microsoft Excel 2010 Certified
Microsoft Outlook 2010 Certified
Microsoft PowerPoint 2010 Certified
Microsoft Word 2010 Certified
Microsoft OneNote 2010 Certified

You can include your personalized logo on business cards and other personal promotional materials. This logo attests to the fact that you are proficient in the applications or cross-application skills necessary to achieve the certification.

For More Information

To learn more about the Microsoft Office Specialist exams and related courseware, visit:

www.microsoft.com/learning/en/us/certification/mos.aspx

Using This Book to Study for a Certification Exam

The Microsoft Office Specialist (MOS) exams for individual Microsoft Office 2010 programs are practical rather than theoretical. You must demonstrate that you can complete certain tasks rather than simply answering questions about program features. The successful MOS certification candidate will have at least six months of experience using all aspects of the application on a regular basis; for example, using Microsoft OneNote at work to take notes, collaborate with other users, search notebooks, and insert files and other types of content.

Each chapter in this book is divided into sections addressing groups of related skills. Each section includes review information, generic procedures, and practice tasks you can complete on your own while studying. When necessary, practice files are included that you can use to work through the practice tasks. You can practice the procedures in this book by using the practice files supplied or by using your own files. (If you use your own files, keep in mind that functionality in some Office 2010 programs is limited in files created in or saved for earlier versions of the program. When working in such a file, *Compatibility Mode* appears in the program window title bar.)

As a certification candidate, you probably have a lot of experience with the program you want to become certified in. Many of the procedures we discuss in this book will be familiar to you; others might not be. Read through each study section and ensure that you are familiar with not only the procedures included in the section, but also the concepts and tools discussed in the review information. In some cases, graphics depict the tools you will use to perform procedures related to the skill set. Study the graphics and ensure that you are familiar with all the options available for each tool.

Features and Conventions of This Book

If you have worked with a previous version of OneNote or if you need help remembering how to perform a particular task, you can use the detailed table of contents to scan a listing of the topics covered in each chapter and locate specific topics.

You can save time when you use this book by understanding how special instructions, keys to press, buttons to click, and other conventions are indicated in this book.

Convention	Meaning
1 **2**	Numbered steps guide you through step-by-step procedures.
➜	An arrow indicates a procedure that has only one step.
See Also	These paragraphs direct you to more information about a given topic in this book or elsewhere.
Tip	These paragraphs provide a helpful hint or shortcut that makes working through a task easier, or information about other available options.
Interface elements	In procedures, the names of program elements (such as buttons and commands) are shown in bold characters.
Key combinations	A plus sign (+) between two key names means that you must hold down the first key while you press the second key. For example, "press Ctrl+Home" means "hold down the Ctrl key and press the Home key."
User input	In procedures, anything you should enter appears in bold italic characters.

Using the Book's Companion Content

Before you can complete the exercises in this book, you need to copy the book's practice files to your computer. These practice files, and other information, can be downloaded from here:

http://go.microsoft.com/FWLink/?Linkid=233092

Display the detail page in your web browser and follow the instructions for downloading the files.

> **Important** Microsoft OneNote 2010 is not available from this website. You should purchase and install the program before using this book.

The following table lists the practice files for this book.

Exam 77-853: Microsoft OneNote 2010 Specialist

Chapter	OneNote Notebooks and Other Files
Chapter 1, "Managing the OneNote Environment"	*Report Requirements* *Logo.png* *Travel Notes*
Chapter 2, "Sharing and Collaborating"	*Fall Catalog Production* *Project Notes*
Chapter 3, "Organizing and Finding Notes"	*Budget Planning* *Department Meetings 2011* *OneNote_Printout.docx*
Chapter 4, "Editing and Linking Content in OneNote"	*Budget Planning* *Home Improvements* *Estimate.xlsx* *Proposal.pptx* *Planning Committee* *Home Remodeling Plans*

Modifying the Display of the Ribbon

The goal of the Microsoft Office working environment is to make working with Office documents as intuitive as possible. You work with an Office file and its contents by giving commands to the program in which the document is open. All Office 2010 programs organize commands on a horizontal bar called the ribbon, which appears across the top of an application's program window.

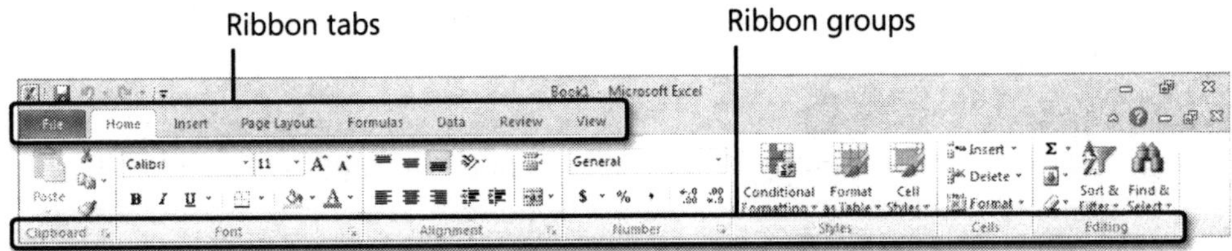

Commands are organized on task-specific tabs of the ribbon, and in feature-specific groups on each tab. Commands generally take the form of buttons and lists. Some appear in galleries. Some groups have related dialog boxes or task panes that contain additional commands.

> **Tip** **Some older commands no longer appear on the ribbon but are still available in the program. You can make these commands available by adding them to the Quick Access Toolbar.**

The appearance of commands on the ribbon changes as the width of the ribbon changes. A command might be displayed on the ribbon in the form of a large button, a small button, a small labeled button, or a list entry. As the width of the ribbon decreases, the size, shape, and presence of buttons on the ribbon adapt to the available space. For example, if you decrease the width of the ribbon, small button labels disappear and entire groups of buttons are hidden under one button that represents the group. Click the group button to display a list of the commands available in that group. When the window becomes too narrow to display all the groups, a scroll arrow appears at its right end. Click the scroll arrow to display hidden groups.

You can customize the ribbon or the Quick Access Toolbar to suit your working style and to make commands you use frequently easily available. To add a command to the Quick Access Toolbar, right-click the command on the ribbon and then choose Add to Quick Access Toolbar.

> **Tip** The screen images shown in the procedures in this book were captured at a screen resolution of 1024 × 768, at 100 percent magnification, and with the default text size (96 dpi). If any of your settings are different, the ribbon on your screen might not look the same as the one shown in the book. If differences between your display settings and ours cause a button on your screen to look different from the one mentioned in this book, you can adapt the procedures to locate the command. First, click the specified tab. Then locate the specified group. If a group has been collapsed into a group list or group button, click the list or button to display the group's commands. Finally, look for a button that features the same icon in a larger or smaller size than that shown in the book. If necessary, point to buttons in the group to display their names in ScreenTips.

To add your own tabs and groups to the ribbon, right-click the ribbon and choose Customize the Ribbon. In the program's Options dialog box (the one shown here is for Word), click New Tab to add a tab to the ribbon. The new tab will include a new group as well. Use the New Group button to add another group to the custom tab or to any of the built-in tabs show in the Main Tabs list. You can add commands only to custom groups, not to any of the built-in groups.

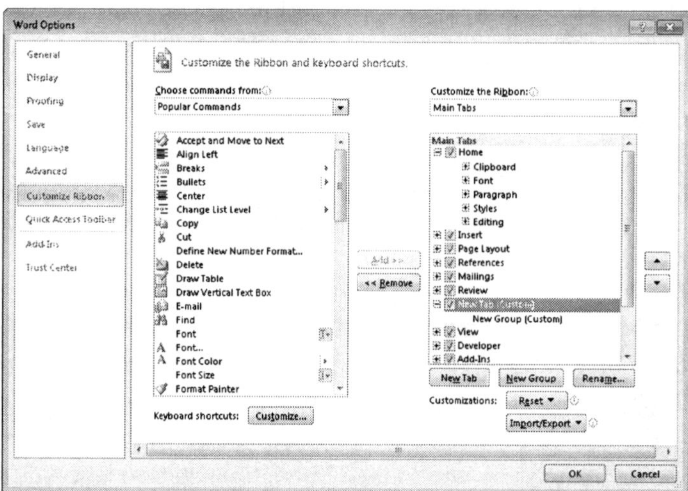

The Choose Commands From list provides options for displaying popular commands, commands not included on the ribbon, as well as all commands or commands on specific tabs. Select the command you want to add to a custom group, and then click Add. Click Remove if you want to remove a command from a custom group.

The Rename button opens a dialog box in which you can type a name for a custom tab or a custom group. For a custom group, you can also select an symbol to associate with the group.

If you want to return the ribbon and the Quick Access Toolbar to the default state, you can click Reset, Reset All Customizations.

Getting Support and Giving Feedback

Errata

We've made every effort to ensure the accuracy of this book and its companion content. Any errors that have been reported since this book was published are listed on our Microsoft Press site at oreilly.com:

http://go.microsoft.com/FWLink/?Linkid=233090

If you find an error that is not already listed, you can report it to us through the same page.

If you need additional support, please send an email message to Microsoft Press Book Support at *mspinput@microsoft.com*.

Please note that product support for Microsoft software is not offered through the addresses above.

Getting Help with Microsoft OneNote 2010

If your question is about Microsoft OneNote 2010, and not about the content of this Microsoft Press book, your first recourse is the Microsoft Office Help system. You can find general or specific Help information in a couple of ways:

- In the program window, you can click the Help button (labeled with a question mark) located in the upper-right corner of the web browser window to display the program-specific Help window.
- In the left pane of the Backstage view, you can click Help to access Microsoft Office Help resources.

If your question is about OneNote 2010 or another Microsoft software product and you cannot find the answer in the product's Help system, please search the appropriate product solution center or the Microsoft Knowledge Base at:

support.microsoft.com/

In the United States, Microsoft software product support issues not covered by the Microsoft Knowledge Base are addressed by Microsoft Product Support Services. Location-specific software support options are available from:

support.microsoft.com/gp/selfoverview/

We Want to Hear from You

At Microsoft Press, your satisfaction is our top priority, and your feedback our most valuable asset. Please tell us what you think of this book at:

www.microsoft.com/learning/booksurvey/

The survey is short, and we read *every one* of your comments and ideas. Thanks in advance for your input!

Stay in Touch

Let's keep the conversation going! We're on Twitter: twitter.com/MicrosoftPress.

Exam 77-853

Microsoft OneNote 2010 Specialist

In this book's four chapters, you'll build on the general skills required to create, manage, and share notebooks in Microsoft OneNote 2010. You'll learn more about the specific skills you need to be certified as a Microsoft OneNote 2010 specialist. The areas covered are the following:

- Manage the OneNote environment
- Sharing and collaborating on notebooks
- Organizing and finding notes
- Editing and linking content in OneNote

What You Need to Know

The skills described in the following chapters cover many of the everyday operations you'll perform when you work in OneNote, including how you create a notebook, share a notebook with other users, organize and search content, and edit and format notes and visual elements such as pictures and drawings. This section provides a brief introduction to OneNote by describing the main elements of a notebook and the elements of the OneNote user interface that you use most often.

OneNote notebooks can be used for any number of purposes—brainstorming sessions, class notes, compiling research, project task assignments and status, and many others. A notebook can contain various types of content—notes you type or write by hand, printouts from files, tables, screen shots, drawings, and pictures are examples.

A notebook contains at least one section, which OneNote includes by default when you create a notebook. You can create additional sections as you need them, and sections can be organized into section groups in a notebook with many sections. Sections contain pages. Pages are where you add notes, pictures, and other types of content. You can also create subpages to define a more detailed level of organization.

Each section in a notebook is saved in a separate file that uses the Microsoft OneNote Section format. These files include the file name extension .one. Section files are stored within a folder that uses the name you assign to a notebook when you create it. (You can change the display name of a notebook if you want to.) Section groups are stored in a subfolder of the notebook's folder. A notebook's folder also includes a file named OpenNotebook.onetoc2. You can double-click this file to open the notebook.

OneNote saves changes you make to a notebook automatically. You don't need to click a Save button or a Save command before you close a notebook, for example.

The following illustration shows the main OneNote window. Open notebooks are listed on the Navigation bar, which appears along the left side of the OneNote window by default. The sections in a notebook are listed under the entry for a notebook in the Navigation bar. Click a section name to display that section. You can also display a section by clicking the section tab that appears across the top of the current page. The pages in a section are listed in the page tabs bar, which is shown along the right side of the window. You can also position the page tabs bar along the left side of the window. Click a page name to display its content. Click New Page at the top of the page tabs bar to insert another page in the section.

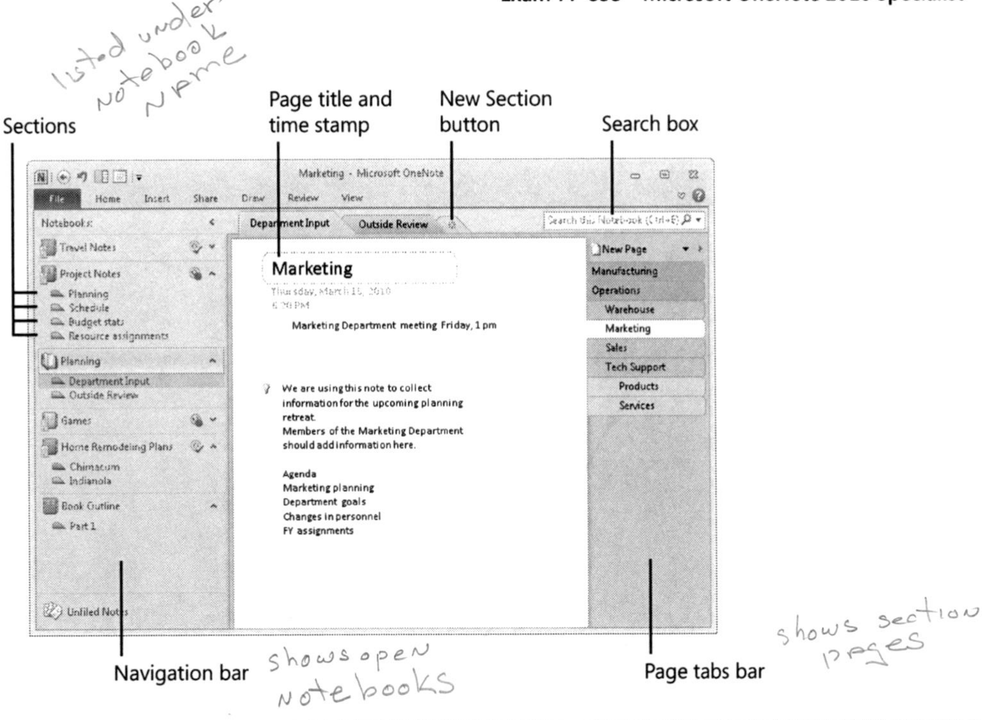

See Also OneNote 2010 provides a number of keyboard shortcuts that let you navigate through a notebook, insert content, and search a notebook for the information you need. You can find a list of the shortcuts in the appendix to this book.

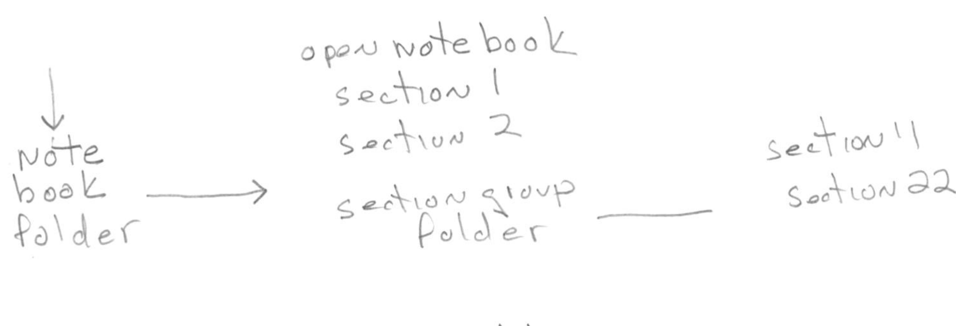

1 Managing the OneNote Environment

The skills tested in this section of the Microsoft Office Specialist exam for Microsoft OneNote 2010 are related to managing the OneNote environment. Specifically, the following objectives are associated with this set of skills:

1.1 Manage page layout
1.2 Configure Backstage view in OneNote
1.3 Create OneNote notebooks
1.4 Personalize OneNote
1.5 Personalize page setup

In this chapter, you'll learn about many of the options and features you use to customize and manage the appearance of notebook pages and the general OneNote workspace. You'll learn about the steps you follow to create a OneNote notebook, which you can store on your own computer, in a network location such as a shared folder or a Microsoft SharePoint site, or on Windows Live SkyDrive. You'll also learn about working with OneNote in Backstage view, which is a feature all Microsoft Office 2010 applications have in common.

1.1 Manage Page Layout

Each page in a OneNote notebook can contain different elements—typewritten notes, handwritten notes, numbered and bulleted lists, tables, images, links to files, and more. Knowing how to move, resize, merge, and split note containers, which are the bounding boxes that enclose each note on a page, is an important aspect of managing page layout. You'll learn how to combine note containers in this section and also how to collapse and expand paragraphs when you need to hide or show information in an outline or a list. In addition, you'll see how to use an image as a page background and how to save a page as a template you can use repeatedly in a single notebook or in any other notebook you create.

Combining Containers

You can drag one note container into another to combine the containers and merge their contents. You might do this to combine notes on a single topic, to add annotations to a picture or a drawing, to create a list or an outline, or to add items to a table.

To merge containers, click the Move handle at the top of the first container to select the container's contents. Hold down the Shift key, and then drag the container to the container you want to combine it with. OneNote highlights the note as you drag it and then displays the borders of the combined container when the notes are merged.

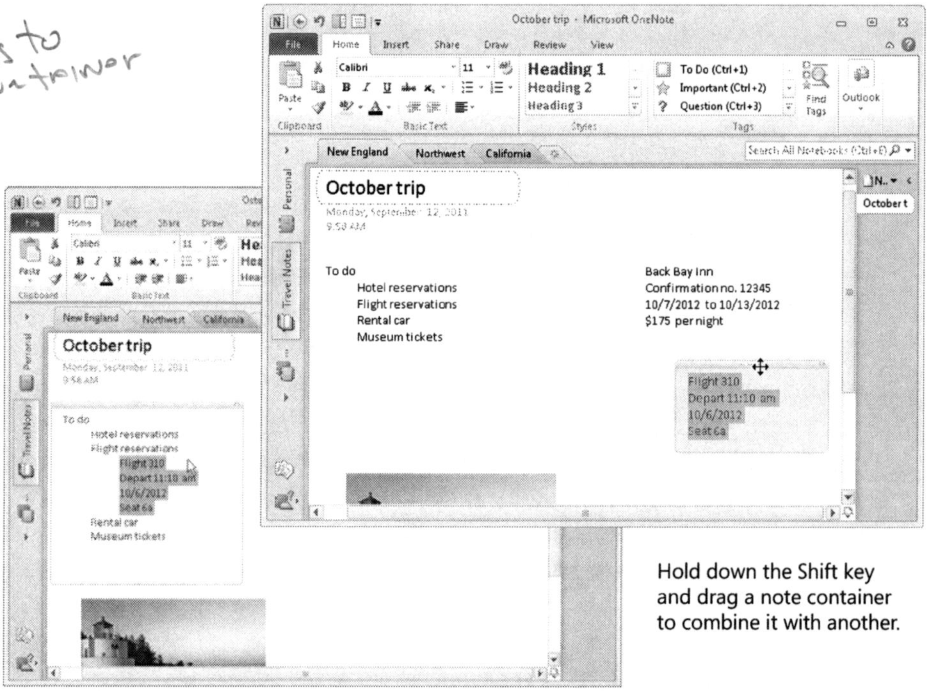

Hold down the Shift key and drag a note container to combine it with another.

> **Tip** To place some of the content in a note in its own container, select the text or other element and then drag it to a new location on the page.

➤ To combine note containers

1. Click the Move handle at the top of the container you want to merge with another container.
2. Hold down the Shift key, and then drag the first container to the second.

Collapsing and Expanding Paragraphs

One of the most effective uses of OneNote is to create outlines for reports, research papers, presentations, and other types of documents. To create an outline (or another type of hierarchical list), add a first-level heading, press Enter to start a new paragraph, and press Tab to indent items under higher-level entries as you complete the outline. (Press Shift+Tab to move back to the next higher level.) If you number the first item (and the option for OneNote to automatically number items in a list is enabled, which is the default setting), OneNote identifies different levels of entries as you work through the outline.

To view an outline at different levels of detail, you can collapse and expand paragraphs. Move the pointer to the left of a paragraph with subheadings under it. You'll see the pointer appear as a four-headed arrow, and OneNote displays a small, similar-looking button next to the item. Double-click the button to collapse or expand the items in the paragraph.

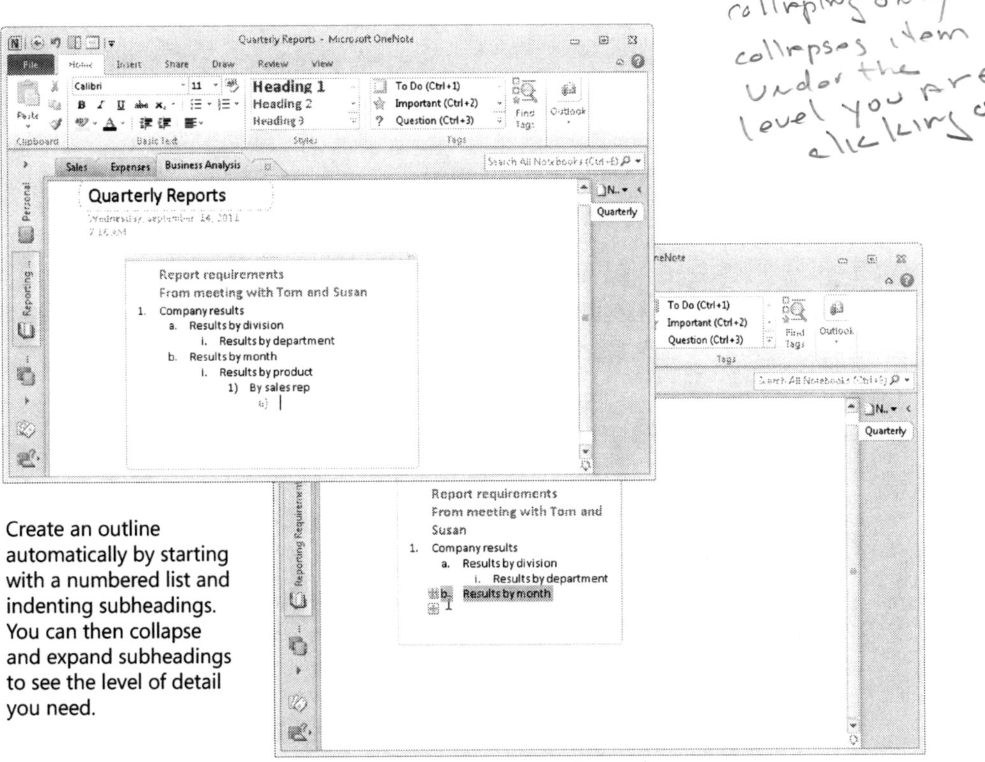

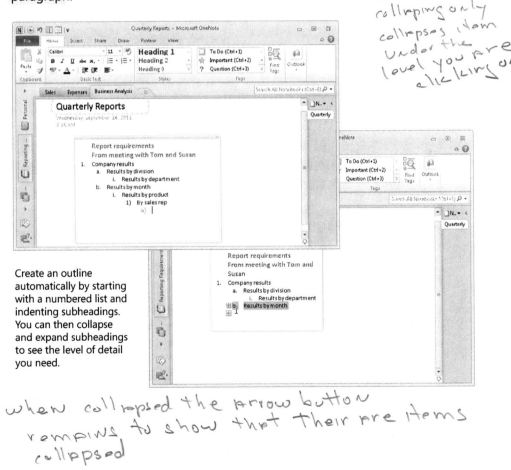

Create an outline automatically by starting with a numbered list and indenting subheadings. You can then collapse and expand subheadings to see the level of detail you need.

You can also use key combinations to work with the paragraphs in an outline. The following table summarizes these keystrokes.

To do this	Press
Show through Level 1.	Alt+Shift+1
Expand to Level 2.	Alt+Shift+2
Expand to Level 3.	Alt+Shift+3
Expand to Level 4.	Alt+Shift+4
Expand to Level 5.	Alt+Shift+5
Expand to Level 6.	Alt+Shift+6
Expand to Level 7.	Alt+Shift+7
Expand to Level 8.	Alt+Shift+8
Expand to Level 9.	Alt+Shift+9
Expand all levels.	Alt+Shift+0
Increase indent by one level.	Tab
Decrease indent by one level.	Shift+Tab
Expand a collapsed outline.	Alt+Shift+plus sign
Collapse an expanded outline.	Alt+Shift+minus sign

➤ To collapse or expand paragraphs

1. Point to the left side of a paragraph with subheadings under it.
2. Double-click the four-headed arrow icon.

   OneNote hides subheadings that are displayed or shows subheadings that were previously collapsed.

Setting an Image as a Background

The background color of a OneNote page is white by default. You can set the background to a different color by using the Page Color option on the View menu. You can also use an image as a background.

> **See Also** For information about the Page Color option, see "Setting Page Properties" later in this chapter.

To set an image as a background, place the image along the top or in the upper-left corner of the page. Also, be sure the image is not placed within a note container. (To remove an image from a note container, select the picture, press Ctrl+X—or choose Cut in the Clipboard group on the Home tab—and then paste the image on the page.)

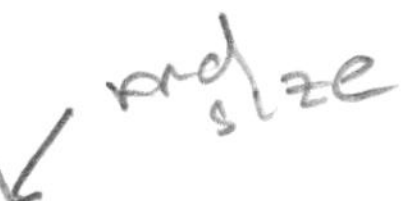

After you insert the image you want to use, right-click the image and choose Set Picture As Background.

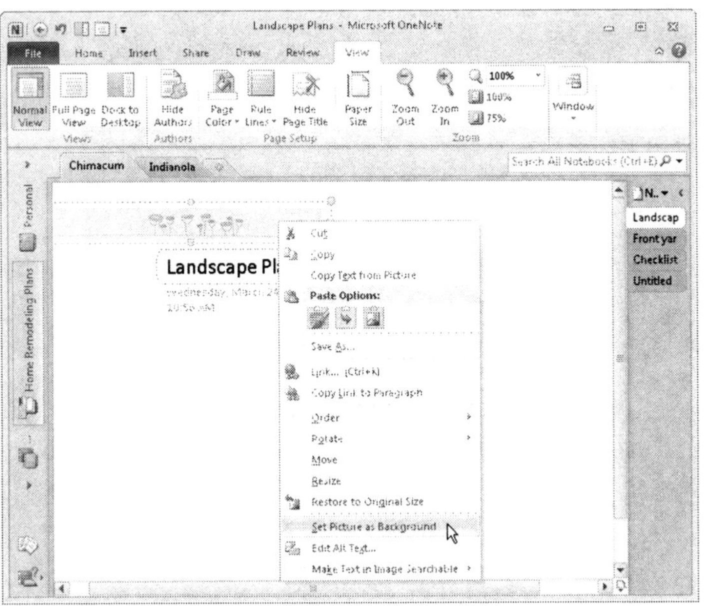

To remove this designation from the image, right-click and clear the Set Picture As Background option. You can then delete the image from the page.

> **Tip** You need to be selective about an image you use as a background so that the image does not obscure notes and other elements you add to a page. Use an image with prominent elements at the top or left and that fades to the right. Look over some of the page templates OneNote provides to see examples of the type of images you might use. For more information about page templates, see the next section.

➤ To set an image as the page background

1. Insert the image you want to use. If necessary, cut and paste the image so that it is not enclosed in a note container.
2. Right-click the image and choose **Set Picture As Background**.

➤ To clear a background image

1. Right-click the background image and then clear the **Set Picture As Background** option.
2. Delete the image.

Saving the Current Page as a Template

OneNote comes with a number of page templates. You can review these templates, which are organized under five default headings (Academic, Blank, Business, Decorative, and Planners), by clicking the down arrow beside New Page in the page tabs bar and then clicking Page Templates. OneNote displays the Templates pane.

Page templates are organized by category. Click the link at the bottom of the Templates pane to save the current page as a custom template.

> **Tip** You can use one of the standard OneNote templates or a page template you create as the default page template for the current section. Open the Templates pane (by clicking Page Templates in the page tabs bar), and then choose the template you want to use from the list under Choose Default Template.

The first step in creating your own page template is to set up the page with the text, images, or other elements you want to work with. If you examine a few of the built-in templates, you can see the types of elements they contain. For example, the Project Overview template, which is included in the Business category, has placeholders for information such as the project name, the project goals and team members, and the schedule.

> **See Also** For more information about editing content in OneNote, including how to insert and modify visual elements, see Chapter 4, "Editing and Linking Content in OneNote." For a list of best practices to use when you create OneNote templates, see the OneNote Help topic "Create a Template in Microsoft Office OneNote 2010."

When the page is ready, open the Templates pane and then click Save Current Page As A Template at the bottom of the pane. In the Save As Template dialog box, type a name for the template. If you want to use this template as the basis for new pages in the current section, select the option to set the page as the default template.

When you save your own page template, OneNote creates a new category, called My Templates, and displays the templates in this group at the top of the Templates pane.

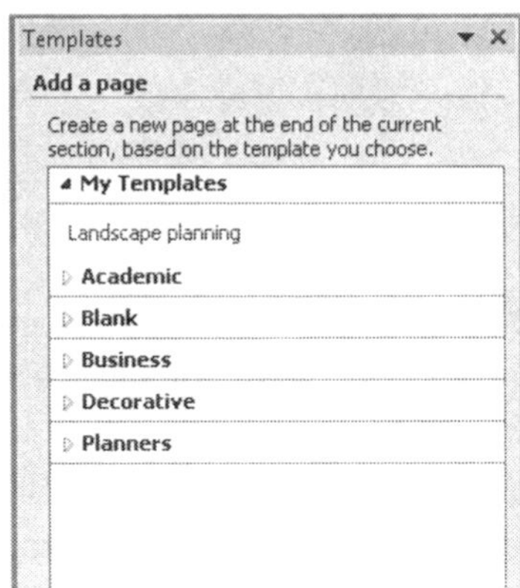

Templates that you define are displayed in the My Templates group at the top of the Templates pane.

➤ To save the current page as a template

1. Set up the page with the elements you want the template to include. These elements might include a page color, an image, or note containers that act as placeholders for specific information.
2. On the page tabs bar, click the arrow next to **New Page**, and then click **Page Templates**.
3. In the **Templates** pane, click **Save Current Page As A Template**.
4. In the **Save As Template** dialog box, type a name for the template.
5. If you want to use this template as the default template for new pages in the current section, select that option and then click **Save**.

Practice Tasks

The files required for this section's practice tasks are located in the practice files folder for Microsoft OneNote 2010. You can change the file name so that you don't overwrite the sample files and save the results of these exercises in the same folder. When you are ready, try performing the following tasks:

- Open OneNote 2010, and open the notebook named Report Requirements.
- On the page named Data Analysis, combine two of the note containers.

- Create a simple outline, and then practice collapsing and expanding paragraphs.
- Create a new page, insert the file Logo.png, and set this image as the page background.
- Save the page with the logo as a page template.

1.2 Configure Backstage View in OneNote

Backstage view is a feature in all Office 2010 programs. This view appears when you click the File tab on the ribbon. Backstage view contains commands such as Info, Open, Save, Save As, Print, and Options. In many Office 2010 applications, including OneNote, you can use the Info page in Backstage view to select settings and specify properties. In the two sections that follow, you'll learn more about some of the ways you work with OneNote in Backstage view.

Configuring Notebook Settings and Properties

Among the notebook settings and properties you can configure are a notebook's display name, the color of the icon it displays in the Navigation bar, its location, and whether the notebook is shared. On the Info page in Backstage view, you can view the current settings for a notebook and update settings and properties when you need to. The Info page lists each open notebook under the heading Notebook Information. The information includes the notebook's display name, its location, and (for shared notebooks) its status. To manage a notebook's settings and properties, you use the Settings button or the links OneNote provides. (The links let you perform some of the same operations available through the Settings button.)

Click the Settings button, and you'll see several items—Share, Close, and Properties for notebooks stored on your computer, and Invite People, Sync, Close, and Properties for notebooks that are shared on the web or on a network.

See Also For information about working with shared notebooks, including how to send invitations and how to synchronize notebooks, see Chapter 2, "Sharing and Collaborating."

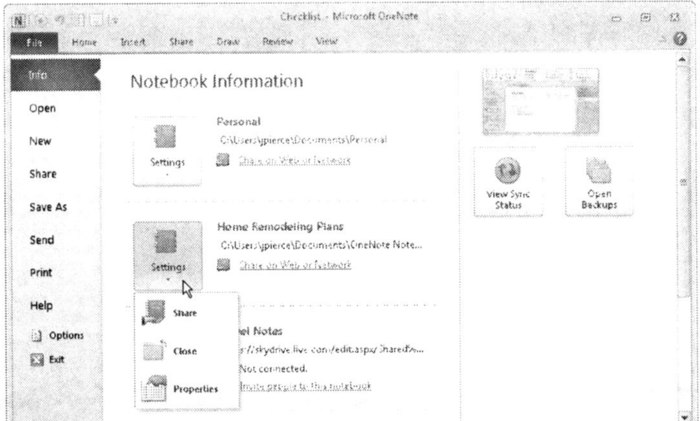

The Info page in Backstage view provides commands and links you can use to configure notebook settings and properties.

If you select the Share option for a local notebook, OneNote switches to the Share page in Backstage view. There you can choose to share the notebook on the web in a Windows Live SkyDrive folder or on a location on your network. If you choose Web under Share On, you then need to sign in to SkyDrive (or sign up for this service if you are a new user).

To share a notebook on a network, click Network and then select one of the recent locations that OneNote lists, type a location in the text box under Network Location, or click Browse and select a network share in the Select Folder dialog box.

See Also **For more information about storing notebooks on the web or on a network location, see "Create OneNote Notebooks" later in this chapter.**

You can close a notebook by clicking Close on the Settings menu. When you choose this command, OneNote returns to the page you were working on in the current notebook. If you close the current notebook, OneNote displays the notebook that appears at the top of the Navigation bar.

The Properties command opens the Notebook Properties dialog box. The first two options in this dialog box let you change a notebook's display name and the color of the icon associated with the notebook. Click Change Location to open a dialog box, named Choose A Sync Location For This Remote Notebook, that you can use to specify a new location for the notebook.

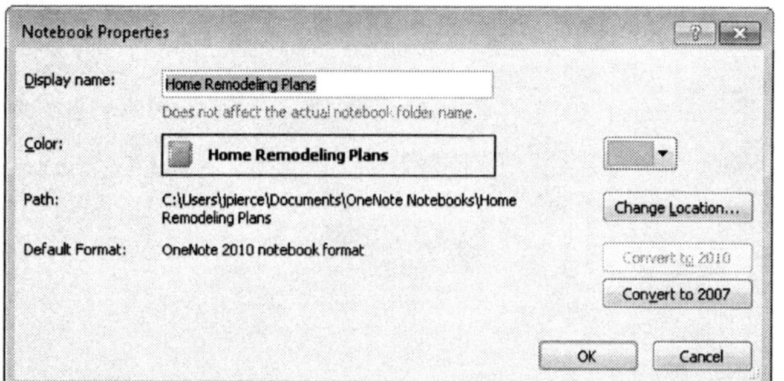

Use the Notebook Properties dialog box to change a notebook's display name, icon color, location, and file format.

> **Tip** You can move a notebook's section files from one folder to another manually, but using the Change Location button in the Notebook Properties dialog box ensures that any sections of a shared notebook will be synchronized after you specify the new location.

Another operation you can perform in the Notebook Properties dialog box is to convert a notebook so that it uses the OneNote 2007 or the OneNote 2010 file format. If you need to share a notebook with someone who uses an earlier version of OneNote, or you want to be able to open a notebook on a computer on which an earlier version of the program is installed, you can use the Convert To 2007 button to save that notebook in the compatible file format. If you convert a notebook to the 2007 format, you can't use all of the features available in OneNote 2010, and some of elements of the notebook will be affected. For example, the math equation feature in OneNote 2010 is not available in the 2007 format. You also cannot use linked notes, and subpages cannot be collapsed under their parent page in the page tabs bar. In addition, the content of a notebook's recycle bin are cleared during conversion.

> **See Also** For more information about linked notes, see "Use Links and Linked Notes" in Chapter 4. For information about the notebook recycle bin, see "Use History and Backups in OneNote" in Chapter 3. Information about working with subpages is provided in "Use OneNote Notebook Organization Tools," also in Chapter 3.

If you want to store a notebook on Windows Live SkyDrive (discussed in "Creating a Notebook on Windows Live SkyDrive" later in this chapter), you need to use the OneNote 2010 format.

➤ To configure and set notebook properties

1. On the ribbon, click **File**, and then click **Info**.
2. Click the **Settings** button for the notebook you want to work with.

3. Click **Properties**.
4. In the **Notebook Properties** dialog box, do the following:
   - Use the **Display Name** box to make changes to the notebook's display name.
   - Select a color for the icon that identifies the notebook in the Navigation bar.
   - Click **Change Location** to move the notebook's file to a different location.
   - Click **Convert To 2007** or **Convert To 2010** to change the notebook's file format.

Pinning Recently Opened Notebooks

Notebooks you have worked with recently (and that you recently closed) are listed in the Recently Closed Notebooks area on the Open page in Backstage view. You can open a notebook by double-clicking the notebook's name.

Notebooks are arranged with the most recently closed notebook first in the list. To move a notebook to the top of the list so that you can find it and open it more quickly, click the pushpin icon. OneNote groups notebooks that you pin in their own group above the other recently closed notebooks.

➤ To pin a notebook

1. Click **File**, **Open**.
2. Under **Recently Closed Notebooks**, click the pushpin icon for a notebook you want to pin to the list.

Practice Tasks

The files required for this section's practice tasks are located in the practice files folder for Microsoft OneNote 2010. You can change the file name so that you don't overwrite the sample files and save the results of these exercises in the same folder. When you are ready, try performing the following tasks:

- Open the notebook named Report Requirements (if it is not already open).
- Use the Notebook Properties dialog box to change the display name for the notebook.
- If you have access to Windows Live SkyDrive or a network location, use the Share option on the Settings menu to share the notebook.

1.3 Create OneNote Notebooks

You create a notebook in Backstage view (on the New page) by providing information in three numbered areas. In the first area, you specify whether to store the notebook on the web, on a network location, or on your local computer. You'll learn more about working with each of these options in the following sections. Next, you type a name for the notebook. OneNote uses this name as the display name for the notebook and for the name of the folder in which the notebook's files are stored. You then specify a particular location—a folder on Windows Live SkyDrive, a network location such as a folder on a server or Microsoft SharePoint site, or a folder on your computer. Click Create Notebook to complete the process.

Tip **You can change the display name for a notebook by right-clicking it in the Navigation bar, clicking Rename (or Properties), and then entering the name in the Notebook Properties dialog box.**

Creating a Notebook on Windows Live SkyDrive

Windows Live SkyDrive is part of the services Microsoft provides through Windows Live. SkyDrive provides free online storage (up to 25 gigabytes) for documents and photos. You can create personal folders on SkyDrive that only you have access to or public folders that you invite others to share.

SkyDrive also lets you create and collaborate on Microsoft Office documents, including OneNote 2010 notebooks, by using Office Web Apps, which are online versions of Microsoft Word, Microsoft Excel, Microsoft PowerPoint, and OneNote. Storing a notebook in a SkyDrive folder is a good plan when you want to have access to it from any computer or you want to share the notebook.

If you have a Windows Live ID (a Hotmail or Live.com e-mail account, for example), you have access to SkyDrive. OneNote also provides a link you can use to sign up for SkyDrive if you want to store a notebook on the web.

See Also **You can learn more about Windows Live services, including SkyDrive, at *www.live.com*. For more information about Office Web Apps, go to *www.office.microsoft.com/web-apps*.**

To begin, click File, New, and then select Web under Store Notebook On. Type a name for the notebook, and then, under Web Location, click Sign In (assuming you have a Windows Live ID).

In the dialog box that appears, type your user name and password and click Sign In. OneNote contacts the server that hosts Windows Live SkyDrive and then displays a list of personal and shared folders. You can create a new shared folder at this point or select one of the folders already defined. Use the Refresh Folder List button to see any updates you make to the group of folders.

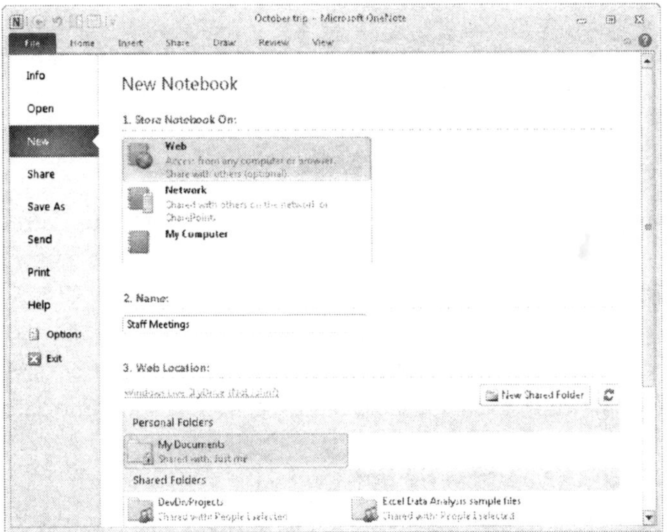

You create a notebook in three steps. This example shows a notebook being created on the web in a Windows Live SkyDrive folder.

Click Create Notebook. After OneNote creates the notebook in the SkyDrive folder, it displays a message box that informs you the notebook is available to anyone who has permissions to access the SkyDrive folder you designated. The message box also prompts you to send a link via e-mail to people you want to invite to share the notebook.

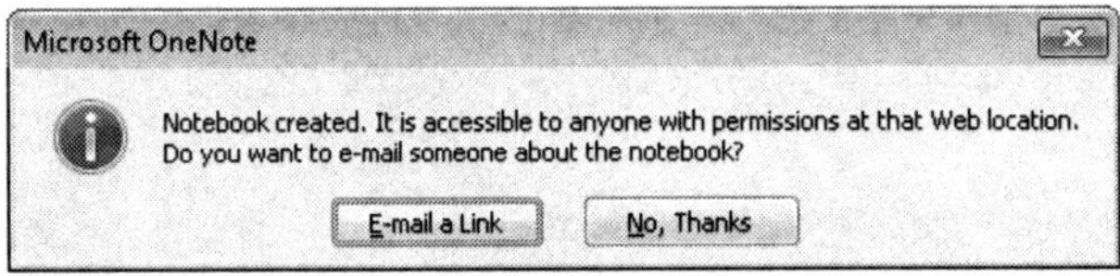

OneNote displays this message box after it creates a notebook on the web or in a network location. You can use the E-Mail A Link button to invite other users to share a notebook.

➤ To create a notebook on the web

1. Click **File**, **New**, and then select **Web** under **Store Notebook On**.
2. Type a name for the notebook.
3. Under **Web Location**, click **Sign In**, and then enter your user name and password for Windows Live SkyDrive.

4. Select a folder currently defined on Windows Live SkyDrive, or click **New Shared Folder**.

   If you create a new shared folder, you need to sign in to Windows Live again, create the folder in your web browser, and then refresh the list of folders displayed in OneNote.

5. Click **Create Notebook**.
6. In the message box OneNote displays, click **E-Mail A Link** to invite others to share the notebook, or click **No, Thanks** to close the message box.

Creating a Notebook on a Network

Storing a notebook on a network location lets you share the notebook with other people in your organization, with your workgroup, with family members—anyone who has permission that provides access to the location you select. Network locations include Microsoft SharePoint sites, so if you are using SharePoint to collaborate with others on a project, adding OneNote notebooks to document libraries on your team site can be an excellent tool for storing notes and compiling and tracking project information.

➤ To create a notebook on a network location

1. Click **File**, **New**, and then select **Network** under **Store Notebook On**.
2. Type a name for the notebook.
3. Under **Network Location**, type the path to the network location, click **Browse** to select the location by using the **Select Folder** dialog box, or select a location you used recently from the list OneNote displays.
4. Click **Create Notebook**.
5. In the message box OneNote displays, click **E-Mail A Link** to invite others to share the notebook, or click **No, Thanks** to close the message box.

Creating a Notebook on Your Computer

The My Computer option in the Store Notebook On list creates a notebook in the default location on your computer. Unless you change the default notebook location in the OneNote Options dialog box, this location is C:\Users*Username*\Documents\OneNote Notebooks (on Windows Vista or Windows 7). If you want to store the notebook you are creating in a different folder, click the Browse button and then use the Select Folder dialog box to designate the folder.

Tip To change the default location for storing notebooks on your computer, click File, Options. In the OneNote Options dialog box, select the Save & Backup page. Under Save, select Default Notebook Location, click Modify, and then select the folder you want to use.

➤ To create a notebook on your computer

1. Click **File**, **New**, and then select **My Computer** under **Store Notebook On**.
2. Type a name for the notebook.
3. Under **Location**, type the path where you want to store the notebook, or click **Browse** to use the **Select Folder** dialog box.
4. Click **Create Notebook**.

Practice Tasks

No sample files are used for this set of practice tasks. To practice the skills described in this section, perform the following tasks:

- Create a notebook on your own computer.
- If you have access to a network or to Windows Live SkyDrive, practice creating notebooks in those locations as well.

1.4 Personalize OneNote

To personalize OneNote, you make settings in the OneNote Options dialog box, which you open by clicking the File tab and then clicking Options. The dialog box (as it does in other Microsoft Office applications) provides several pages on which you select and configure options that control, for example, which misspellings OneNote corrects automatically, how OneNote displays pages by default, and which language settings you use. OneNote also provides options for working in the Research pane and for specifying how it translates text.

See Also For information about working in the Research pane, including how to translate text in OneNote, see "Conducting Research" in Chapter 4.

Working in the OneNote Options Dialog Box

In the following sections, you'll learn more about options for personalizing OneNote that are included in the OneNote Options dialog box.

Setting the Default Font and Size

On the General page of the OneNote Options dialog box, the Default Font area includes three settings. Use the Font list to select the font you want OneNote to display by default when you type a note. OneNote uses the font you select, but in a larger size, for page titles. The Size list controls the default font size for notes, and the Font Color list provides a palette of color choices. Click More Colors at the bottom of the color palette to open the Colors dialog box, where you can choose from additional colors or define a custom color.

Configuring Display Settings

A list of nine options appears on the Display page.

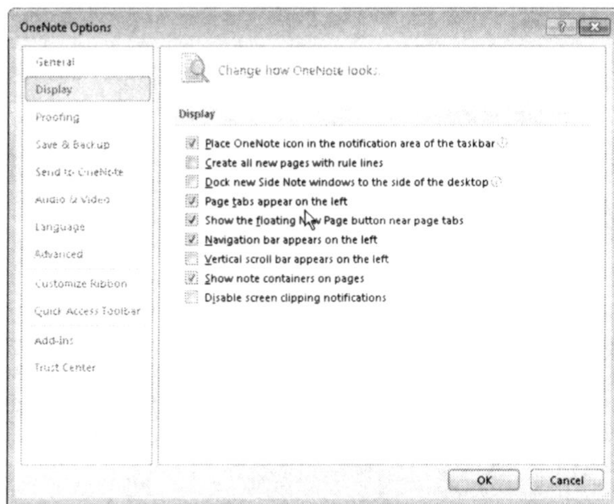

The following six options are selected by default:

- **Place OneNote Icon In The Notification Area Of The Taskbar** You can click this icon to create a side note (which you'll learn more about in "Use OneNote Notebook Organization Tools" in Chapter 3), or right-click the icon and select from a menu of options, as shown.

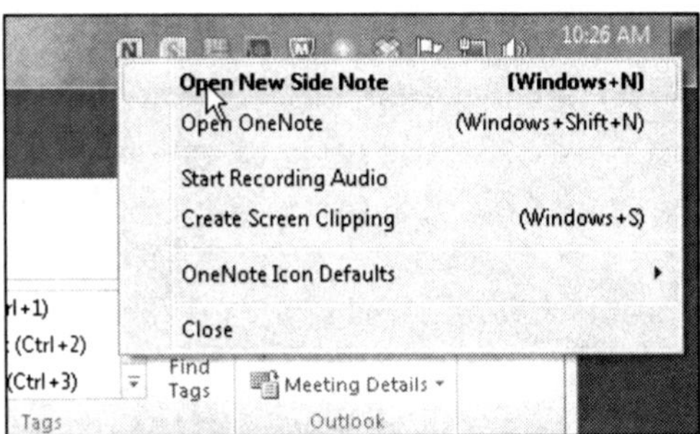

By default, OneNote displays an icon in the notification area of the Windows task bar. Use the OneNote Icon Defaults command to change the action that occurs when you click the icon.

Click OneNote Icon Defaults to change the action that occurs when you click the icon, which is to open a new side note by default. Other options you can choose from are to open OneNote, start an audio recording, or create a screen clipping.

- **Page Tabs Appear On The Left** Clear this option to display the page tabs at the right side of the OneNote window.
- **Show The Floating New Page Button Near Page Tabs** Clear this option to hide the floating New Page button.
- **Navigation Bar Appears On The Left** Clear this setting to display the Navigation bar on the right.
- **Show Note Containers On Pages** Clear this option to hide note containers when you select a note.
- **Disable Screen Clipping Notifications** One of the elements you can add to a notebook is a clipping from a window open on your screen. You might create a screen clipping to add an image from a website to a notebook page, or to include a section of a Microsoft Word document or a drawing in Microsoft Visio. If you want OneNote to display a notification that describes the steps you follow to create a screen clipping, clear this option.

You can also set three other options on the Display page:

- **Create All New Pages With Rule Lines** For more information about working with rule lines on pages, see "Setting Page Properties" later in this chapter.
- **Dock New Side Note Windows To The Side Of The Desktop** By default, the side note window is a floating window. Select this option to dock the side note window to the desktop.
- **Vertical Scroll Bar Appears On The Left** The vertical scroll bar you use to move up and down the current page appears on the right side of the page by default. Select this option to display it on the left.

Specifying Proofing Settings

The Proofing page in the OneNote options dialog box is divided into three areas. In the first of these, click the AutoCorrect Options button to open the AutoCorrect dialog box. In OneNote 2010, the AutoCorrect dialog box has two tabs: AutoCorrect and Math AutoCorrect. Use the AutoCorrect tab to specify whether OneNote should automatically correct two initial capital letters, for example, or always capitalize the names of days. You can also add to the built-in list of misspelled words and character combinations that OneNote replaces automatically with the correct spelling or a corresponding symbol.

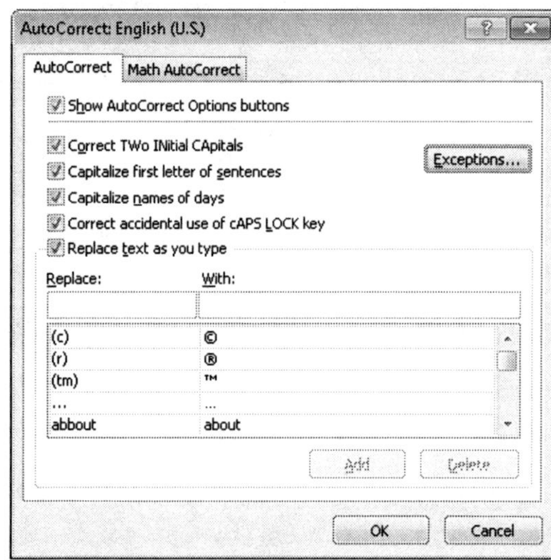

As in other Office applications, you can define the typographic corrections OneNote makes automatically, including correcting misspelled words and replacing character combinations with symbols.

Click the Exceptions button to open a dialog box in which you can define combinations of two capital letters that OneNote won't correct (IDs is defined as an exception by default) as well as abbreviations that end in a period (such as Blvd.), after which OneNote won't capitalize the next character.

On the Math AutoCorrect tab of the AutoCorrect dialog box, you can define character combinations that you type to produce mathematical symbols in equations. For example, if you type the character sequence **\neq** (for "not equal") within the field for an equation, OneNote inserts the symbol ≠.

In the other areas on the Proofing page, you can set options for how all Office programs correct spelling and whether OneNote checks spelling as you type and whether it hides spelling errors.

Working with Language Settings

The Language page lets you specify language settings for all Office programs—in other words, any changes you make to this page affect not only OneNote but Word, Excel, PowerPoint, and the other Office applications you have installed. You can set up additional editing languages (the languages Office takes into account when it checks the spelling or the grammar in a notebook and when it sorts text). You can also choose the language Office uses for displaying the names of commands on the ribbon and in the Help files. (Click the link to Office.com to learn how to get additional display languages.) In this page's third section, you can change the language used to display ScreenTips. You can choose the option to match the display language or choose an alternative from the list. Here again, you can click a link to a page on Office.com to learn how to obtain more ScreenTip languages.

Setting Advanced Options

Many of the options on the Advanced page of the OneNote Options dialog box are related to specific features that are described in more detail in other chapters of this book:

- **Linked Notes** See "Use Links and Linked Notes" in Chapter 4.
- **E-Mail Sent From OneNote** See "E-Mailing Pages in Shareable Formats" in Chapter 2.
- **Tags** See "Configuring Tag Options" in Chapter 3.
- **Passwords** See "Protecting Sections with a Password" in Chapter 3.
- **Search** See "Search OneNote" in Chapter 3.
- **Pen** See "Using and Setting Pen Options" in Chapter 4.

The options in the Editing section of the Advanced page are all selected by default. You can clear these options to do the following:

- Hide the Paste Options button when you paste content
- Not include a link to the source of content you paste into OneNote from the web
- Turn off the automatic creation of numbered and bulleted lists
- Turn off the automatic calculation of mathematical calculations
- Turn off the creation of links that you create by typing double brackets ([[ ]]) around a phrase.

➤ To specify settings in the OneNote Options dialog box

1. On the ribbon, click **File**, and then click **Options**.
2. In the **OneNote Options** dialog box, click the category for the options you want to set.
3. Select check boxes for the options you want to enable, or clear the check boxes for options you want to turn off.

Configuring Research and Translation Options

The Research command and the Translate command appear on the OneNote ribbon's Review tab. Click Research to open the Research pane (which is available also in other Office applications). The Research pane provides a search box you can use to find information in reference books, via research sites such as Bing, and on business and financial websites. You can add to the sources OneNote uses, remove or update these sources, and set parental controls (if necessary) in the Research Options dialog box, which OneNote displays when you click the Research Options link at the bottom of the Research pane.

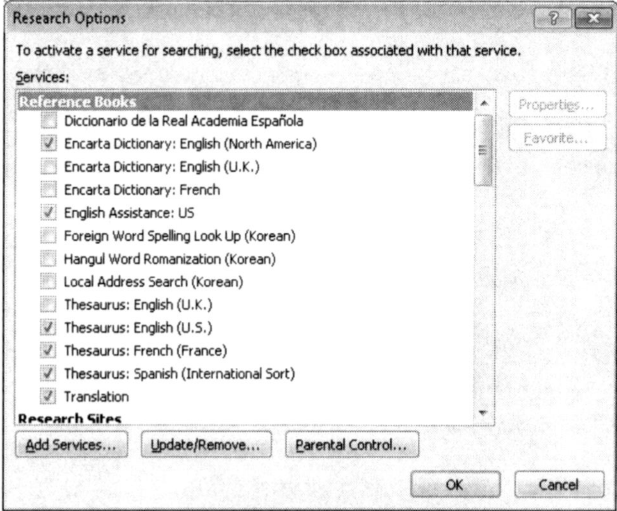

Tip If you click Parental Control in the Research Options dialog box, you are likely to see a message box that indicates you do not have permission to change these settings. If you need to work with parental controls in OneNote, close the program, and then navigate on your computer to the folder Program Files\Microsoft Office\Office 14. Locate the file Onenote.exe, right-click the file, and choose Run As Administrator. Enter administrator account credentials if needed. Return to the Research Options dialog box to set options for parental controls.

When you click Translate, Choose Translation Language, OneNote displays the Translation Language Options dialog box. Use this dialog box to select the language OneNote and other Office applications use when you run the mini translator to translate text.

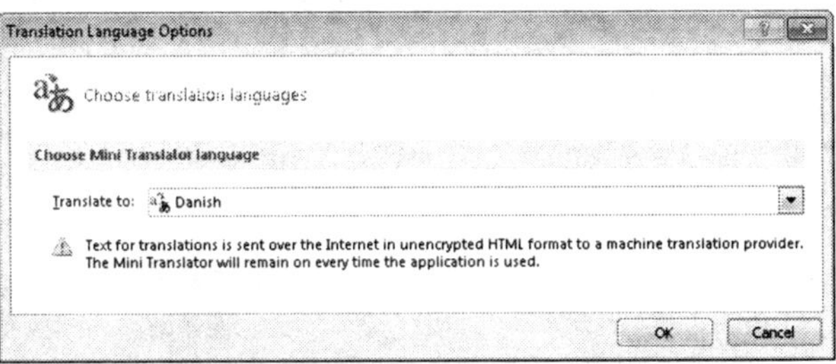

See Also You'll learn the details of how to translate text in "Conducting Research" in Chapter 4.

➤ To set research options

1. On the **Review** tab, click **Research**.
2. At the bottom of the **Research** pane, click **Research Options**.
3. Use the **Research Options** dialog box to update services, add or remove services, and make settings for parental controls.

➤ To set translation options

1. On the **Review** tab, click **Choose Translation Language**.
2. In the **Translation Language Options** dialog box, choose the language you want to use.

Practice Tasks

No sample files are used for this set of practice tasks. To practice the skills described in this section, perform the following tasks:

- Open OneNote, and experiment with some of the settings in the OneNote Options dialog box described in this section to see how they change the appearance and operation of OneNote.
- Use the Display page in the OneNote Options dialog box to reposition the Navigation bar and the page tabs, and see which orientation best fits your working style.
- Change the default font and font color for notes.

1.5 Personalize Page Setup

You can change how pages are set up in OneNote to assist you in the work you are doing. For example, use a blank page with no background color for sketches and drawings, or apply a different page color to identify the pages in a section. If you are taking notes by using a pen, you can set up a page with ruled lines, or you can display a grid pattern to help create floor plans or other types of drawings that need to show precise proportions and scale.

OneNote also provides options for how to view pages. In Normal view, you see the Navigation bar and the page tabs bar. In Full Page view, OneNote hides these navigational components so that you see more of the page. If you want to work with OneNote and another application simultaneously, you can dock the OneNote window to the desktop. By choosing the command to dock the OneNote window, you also enable linked notes, which you'll learn about in detail in Chapter 4.

Setting Page Properties

The Page Setup group on the View tab includes four commands you can use to set page properties:

- **Page Color** Click Page Color and then select one of the 16 options for a colored background. Click No Color to use the default white background.
- **Rule Lines** The Rule Lines command provides options for adding ruled lines or a grid to pages. You can choose from four styles of ruled lines (narrow, college, standard, and wide) or from four options for a grid (small, medium, large, and very large). Choose None to use an unlined page.

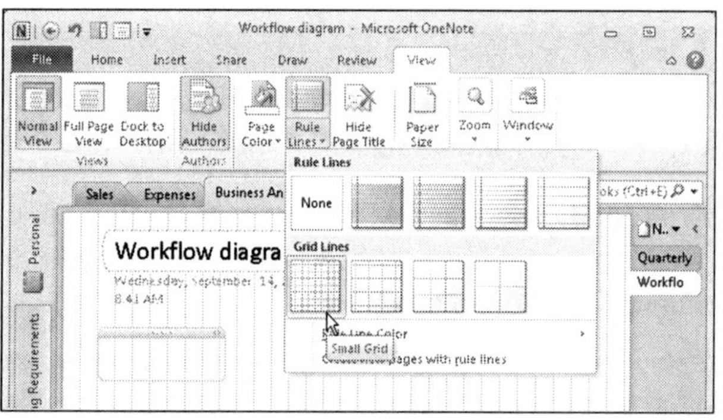

When you need to add ruled lines or a grid to a page, choose an option from the Rule Lines gallery on the View tab.

Ruled lines appear in light blue by default. To choose a different color, click Rule Lines, Rule Line Color, and then select one of the options from the list. If you want to include ruled lines on new pages, select that option on the Rule Lines menu. Clear the option to create unlined pages.

- **Hide Page Title** Use the Hide Page Title command to specify whether OneNote displays the page title in the upper-left corner of a page.
- **Paper Size** Click the Paper Size command to display a task pane in which you can select a standard paper size (or return to the Auto option that OneNote uses by default), set the width and height of the paper size, choose an orientation (portrait or landscape), and specify settings for margins along the top and bottom and the left and right sides of the page. OneNote applies the settings for margins when you print a page. Choose the Custom option at the bottom of the Size list to define a paper size of your own.

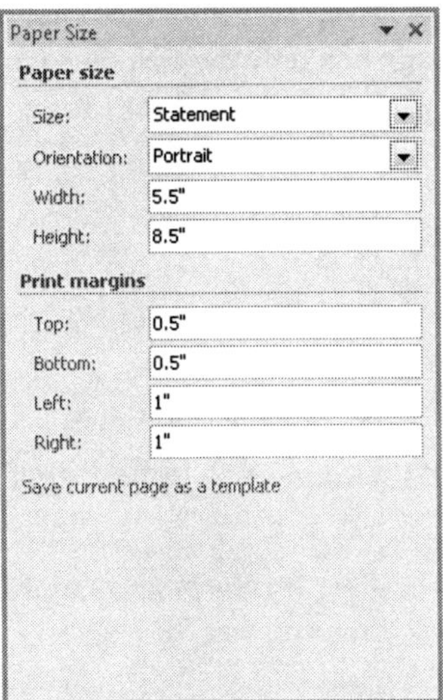

Choose a built-in paper size (such as Statement, shown here), or choose Custom from the Size list and define your own settings for width, height, and print margins.

> **See Also** The Paper Size task pane also includes the link Save Current Page As A Template. For information about saving a page as a template, see "Saving the Current Page as a Template" earlier in this chapter.

➤ To add a page color

1. On the ribbon, click the **View** tab.
2. In the **Page Setup** group, click **Page Color**, and then select the color you want to apply.
3. Click **No Color** to use the default white background.

➤ To add ruled lines to a page

1. On the ribbon, click the **View** tab.
2. In the **Page Setup** group, click **Rule Lines**.
3. In the **Rule Lines** or **Grid Lines** group, select the style you want to use.
4. To apply a color to ruled lines you've added to a page, click **Rule Line Color** and then select a color.

➤ To hide the page title

1. On the ribbon, click the **View** tab.
2. In the **Page Setup** group, click **Hide Page Title**.
3. If OneNote displays a message box prompting you to confirm this action, click **Yes**.

> **Note** You need to click Yes in the message box only the first time you choose Hide Page Title in a notebook.

4. To show the page title again, click **Hide Page Title**.

➤ To specify a page size

1. On the ribbon, click the **View** tab.
2. In the **Page Set Up** group, click **Paper Size**.
3. In the **Paper Size** pane, choose one of the paper size options that OneNote provides or choose **Custom**.
4. Change the settings for the page orientation, its width and height, and print margins.
5. Close the **Paper Size** pane.

Docking the OneNote Window and Managing OneNote Views

In the Views group on the OneNote ribbon's View tab, you can switch from Normal view to Full Page view. In Full Page view, OneNote does not display the Navigation bar or the page tabs bar. You still see the tab names across the top of the ribbon, but OneNote collapses the ribbon when you first switch to Full Page view. To expose the ribbon, click the Expand The Ribbon button (the heart-shaped icon) near the end of the ribbon on the right.

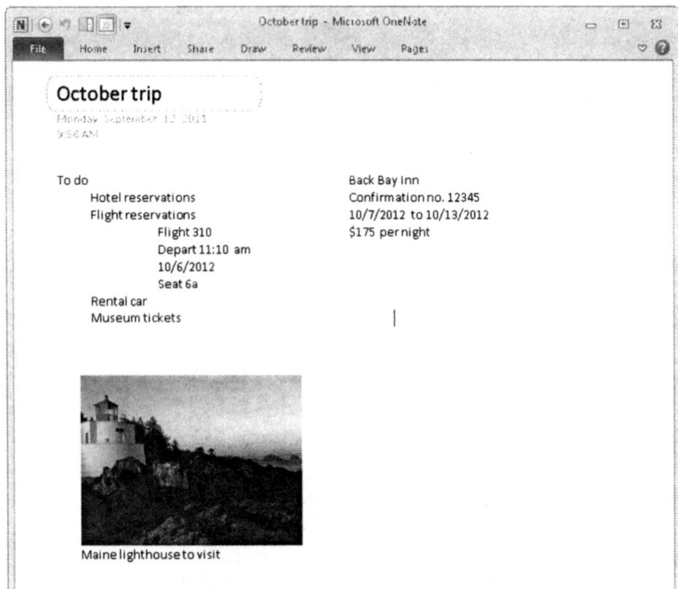

In Full Page view, OneNote hides the Navigation bar and the page tabs bar so that you can see more of the page.

The Dock To Desktop command anchors the OneNote window to the desktop, along the right side of the screen by default. You can drag the docked window to the left side or the top of the screen. When you choose Dock To Desktop, you also enable linked notes, which is indicated by the linked-chain icon OneNote displays in the top-left corner of the window. Click Stop Taking Linked Notes to turn off this feature, or click Linked Notes Options to open the area of the OneNote Options dialog box where you set options for using the feature.

> **See Also** You'll learn about the details of linked notes in "Use Links and Linked Notes" in Chapter 4.

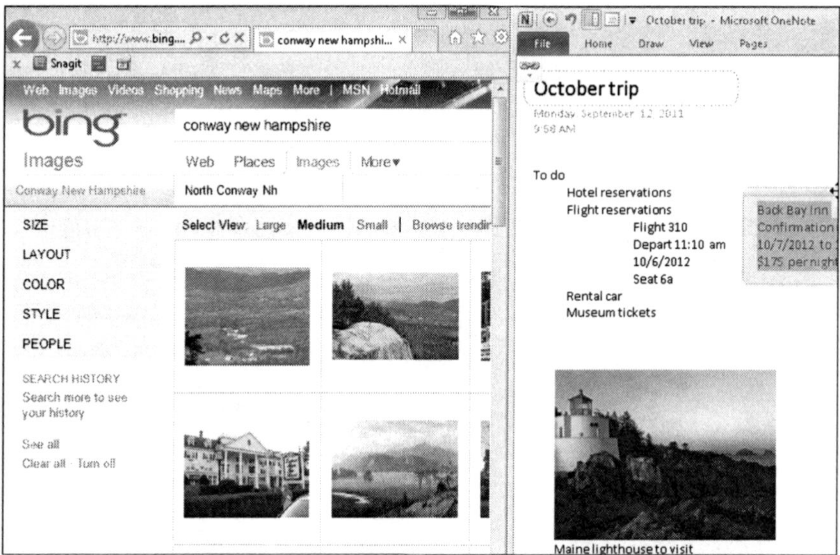

You can dock the OneNote window to the desktop to create notes linked to a web page or another type of document.

> **Tip** In the Window group on the View tab, OneNote includes the New Docked Window command. Click this command to display the current page in a separate window (and enable linked notes).

> **See Also** To learn more about the Hide Authors command on the View tab, see "Hiding Author Initials" in Chapter 2.

➤ To dock the OneNote window to the desktop

1. On the ribbon, click the **View** tab.
2. In the **Views** group, click **Dock To Desktop**.
3. To reposition the docked window, drag it to the top or to the left side of the screen.

Practice Tasks

The files required for this section's practice tasks are located in the practice files folder for Microsoft OneNote 2010. You can change the file name so that you don't overwrite the sample files and save the results of these exercises in the same folder. When you are ready, try performing the following tasks:

- Open the Travel Notes notebook.
- In the California section, create a new page and then apply a page color and different ruled line styles.
- Hide the page title on the page you created.
- Define a custom paper size that has a portrait orientation and is 6 inches wide by 9 inches in height. Set margins of 1 inch for the top and bottom of the page and 1.5 inches on each side.
- Switch this page to Full Page view and then use the Dock To Desktop view.

Objective Review

Before finishing this chapter, be sure you have mastered the following skills:

- Manage page layout
- Configure Backstage view in OneNote
- Create OneNote notebooks
- Personalize OneNote
- Personalize page setup

2 Sharing and Collaborating

The skills tested in this section of the Microsoft Office Specialist exam for Microsoft OneNote 2010 are related to how you can share a notebook and collaborate with others by using OneNote. Specifically, the following objectives are associated with this set of skills:

- **2.1** Share OneNote notebooks
- **2.2** Share OneNote content via e-mail
- **2.3** Collaborate in OneNote

OneNote 2010 provides many features that support sharing notebooks—notebooks that you need to use yourself on more than one computer, and notebooks that two or more people work on together.

OneNote automatically synchronizes changes to a shared notebook so that the version you are working with on your local computer is current. OneNote also provides a set of tools you can use when you work on a notebook collaboratively. These tools help you locate notes by a specific author or notes that were written last week, since the beginning of last month, or over other periods of time. OneNote also highlights notes you haven't read so that you can see at a glance how the content of a shared notebook has changed.

2.1 Share OneNote Notebooks

As you learned in Chapter 1, "Managing the OneNote Environment," you have the option to share a notebook when you create it. You can choose to share a notebook on the web in a Windows Live SkyDrive folder or in a network location such as a shared folder or a Microsoft SharePoint site. You can also share a notebook later, after you have started to work with it, by using the Settings button on the Info tab in Backstage view.

See Also For more information, see "Create OneNote Notebooks" and "Configure Backstage View in OneNote" in Chapter 1.

Another way to share a notebook is to go directly to the Share page in Backstage view, which you can display by clicking File on the ribbon and then clicking Share or by clicking Share This Notebook on the OneNote ribbon's Share tab. (You can also display the Share page by pressing the keyboard combination Alt, F, E.) In the Share On area, use the Web option to share a notebook on Windows Live SkyDrive. If you want to share a notebook on a Microsoft SharePoint site or in a network location, select Network.

Tip Click New Shared Notebook on the Share tab to display the New page in Backstage view, where you can define a new notebook you want to share.

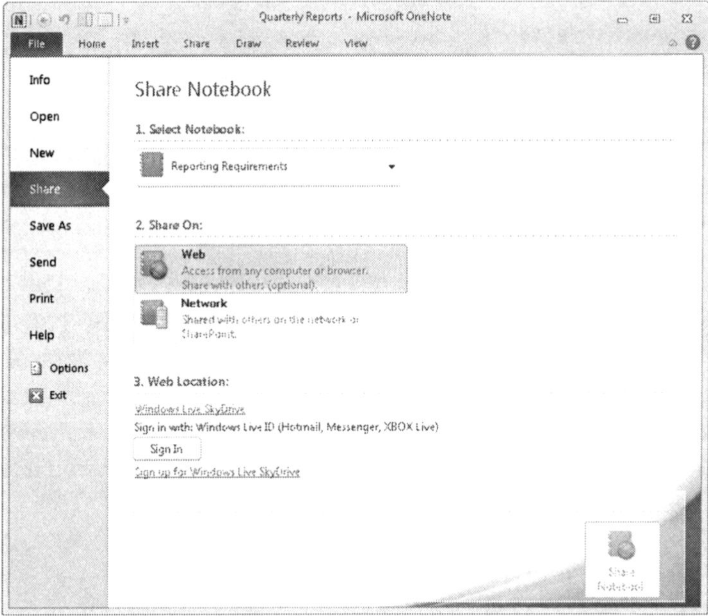

You can share a notebook when you create it, or share a notebook later by using the Share tab in Backstage view.

Tip By sharing a notebook on the web or in a network location, you can access the notebook from more than one computer. For example, you can work with a notebook stored on Windows Live SkyDrive from any computer that can connect to the Internet.

Sharing Notebooks on Windows Live SkyDrive

Sharing a notebook on Windows Live SkyDrive requires four steps (assuming that you have a Windows Live ID, which you need to log on to Windows Live and gain access to Windows Live SkyDrive).

> **See Also** For information about obtaining a Windows Live ID, see *www.live.com*. You can also find information about other Windows Live services on this site.

In most cases, you won't need to change the setting under Select Notebook, but you can select a notebook from this list if you aren't sharing the current notebook. Select Web under Share On, and then click Sign In to log on to SkyDrive. OneNote then displays the folders already defined on the SkyDrive that you logged on to. Select a folder under Shared Folders, or click New Shared Folder to define a folder specifically for this notebook. If you click New Shared Folder, the Windows Live SkyDrive sign-in page opens in your browser. Log on with your Windows Live ID, and then you'll see the Create A Folder page. After typing a name for the folder, click Change to set up the folder so that the users you designate have access to it. You can sign out of Windows Live at this point, and return to OneNote.

> **Important** The services in Windows Live, including Windows Live SkyDrive, are updated from time to time, so the steps described here for working on the Create A Folder page might not apply in every case.

On the Share page in Backstage view, click Refresh to see the updated list of folders. Select the folder you want to use, and then click Share Notebook to complete the process. If you want to send a link about the notebook to another user, click E-Mail A Link in the message box OneNote displays.

➤ To share a notebook on Windows Live SkyDrive

1. On the **Share** tab, click **Share This Notebook**.
2. On the **Share** page, under **Share On**, click **Web**.
3. Under **Network Location**, click **Sign In**, and then sign in by using your Windows Live ID.
4. Click **Share Notebook**.
5. In the message box, click **E-Mail A Link** if you want to send a link to the notebook to other users, or click **No, Thanks**.

Sharing Notebooks on a SharePoint Site

You follow essentially the same set of steps to place a notebook on a SharePoint site, where anyone who has access to the document library in which you save the notebook can open it and use it.

You need to know the address (URL) for the site and the name of the document library in which you want to store the notebook. You can type this information in the Location box when you share the notebook or use the Select Folder dialog box to navigate to the site.

You will probably need to enter the credentials required to log on to the SharePoint site. If you include the root site address in the Network Location box but do not include the name of a valid document library in the path, OneNote opens the Select Folder dialog box after you click Browse. You can use the dialog box to select the folder (library) in which to store the notebook.

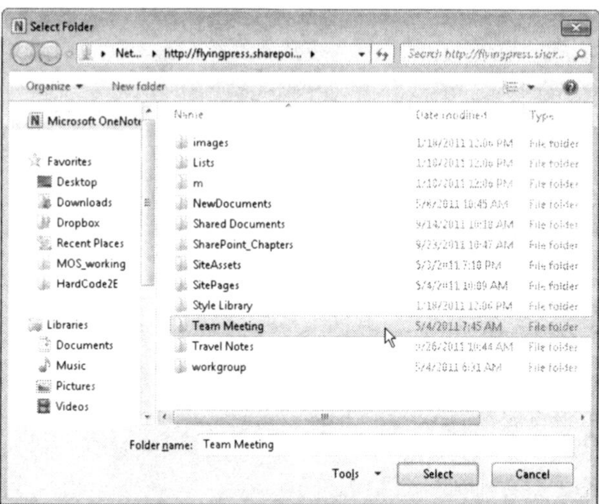

If you don't know the full URL for the document library on a SharePoint site you want to use for a shared notebook, type the site address on the Share page and then use the Select Folder dialog box to specify the library.

OneNote displays a message box after you click Share Notebook. You can use this message box to send a link to the notebook to other users via e-mail.

> **See Also** For more information about notifying other users about a shared notebook via e-mail, see "E-Mailing Others About the Notebook" and "Inviting Others to View a Notebook" later in this chapter.

➤ **To share a notebook on a SharePoint site**

1. On the **Share** tab, click **Share This Notebook**.
2. On the **Share** page, under **Share On**, click **Network**.
3. Under **Network Location**, type the path to the network location, or click **Browse** to open the **Select Folder** dialog box, select the folder in the dialog box, and then click **Select**. You might need to enter your user name and password for the SharePoint site before OneNote displays the dialog box.
4. Click **Share Notebook**.
5. In the message box, click **E-Mail A Link** if you want to send a link to the notebook to other users, or click **No, Thanks**.

Sharing Notebooks on a Network Drive

When you want to share a notebook on a network drive, you first need to know the path to the location in which you want to locate the notebook. You must have permissions to access this site (at a level that grants you permission to store files in that location). Select Network under Share On, type the path in the Network Location box (or use the Browse button to select the location from the Select Folder dialog box). You can also select any of the recent locations that OneNote displays. Click Share Notebook to complete the process, and then use the message box that OneNote displays to send a link to the notebook to the people you want to share the notebook with.

Keep in mind that notifying people of a notebook's location—inviting them to share the notebook—doesn't automatically grant the recipients access to the network location in which you saved the notebook. Permissions to network locations are administered separately and must be updated if necessary to grant access to people who need to work with the notebook.

➤ **To share a notebook on a network drive**

1. On the **Share** tab, click **Share This Notebook**.
2. On the **Share** page, under **Share On**, click **Network**.
3. Under **Network Location**, type the path to the network location, or click **Browse** to open the **Select Folder** dialog box, select the folder in the dialog box, and then click **Select**.
4. Click **Share Notebook**.
5. In the message box, click **E-Mail A Link** if you want to send a link to the notebook to other users, or click **No, Thanks**.

Synchronizing Shared Notebooks

Shared notebooks are identified in the Navigation bar by a Sync Status icon. The icon displays a symbol to indicate the status of synchronization. For example, you'll see a check mark when a notebook is up to date. You'll see a warning exclamation mark when OneNote has encountered problems with the synchronization process (for example, if some sections are not available or in a location that is not accessible.) The icon shows arrows spinning in a circle when a notebook is being synchronized.

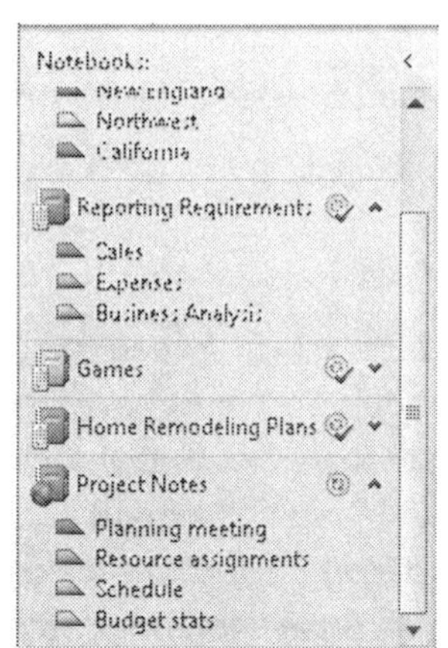

Refer to the icons beside a notebook's name in the Navigation bar to determine the notebook's synchronization status.

When you share a notebook on the web, on a SharePoint site, or in a network location, OneNote keeps a local copy of the shared notebook, which lets you work with the most up-to-date copy (the most recently synchronized version) when you are offline and away from the network. OneNote synchronizes changes to shared notebooks (made by you or by people with whom you share the notebook) when you connect to the network or the Internet (you might need to enter a user name and password), which makes the local copy and the shared copy the same.

To be sure that a shared notebook is current—that all the most recent changes are available to you to review—you can use the synchronization feature in OneNote. You can begin synchronization in a number of ways. You can right-click a notebook in the Navigation bar and click Sync This Notebook Now. You can also display the Info page in Backstage view, click Settings for the notebook you want to synchronize, and then click Sync. To start synchronizing a notebook by using the keyboard, select a section of the notebook in the Navigation bar and then press Shift+F9. You can also right-click a notebook, click Notebook Sync Status, select the notebook in the Shared Notebook Synchronization dialog box, and then click Sync Selected Notebook.

Tip You can synchronize all opens notebooks by pressing F9.

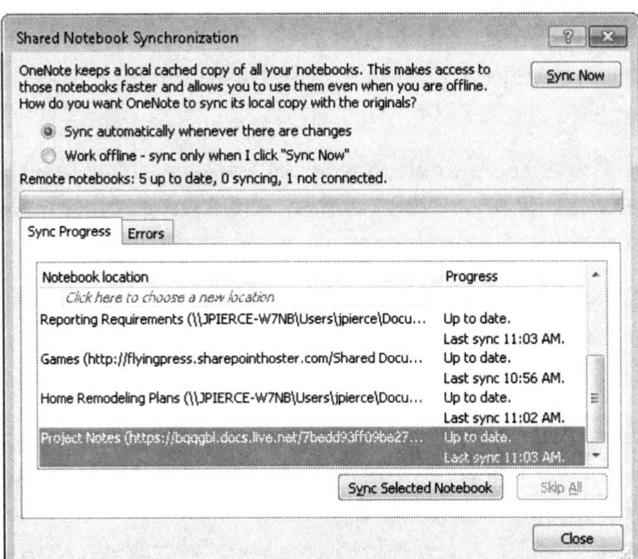

Control when OneNote synchronizes notebooks by setting the options at the top of this dialog box. Click Sync Now to synchronize all notebooks, or select a notebook and then click Sync Selected Notebook.

If you want to control when synchronization occurs (instead of having OneNote synchronize changes automatically), select the option Work Offline—Sync Only When I Click "Sync Now" at the top of the Shared Notebook Synchronization dialog box.

Practice Tasks

No sample files are used for this set of practice tasks. To practice the skills described in this section, perform the following tasks:

- If you have access to Windows Live SkyDrive, a SharePoint site, or a network location, open OneNote and share one of your own notebooks.
- Make changes to the notebook, and then use the synchronization features in OneNote to bring the shared notebook up to date.

2.2 Share OneNote Content via E-Mail

By knowing how to use e-mail to share information you store in OneNote, you can distribute that information to users who don't have OneNote or aren't familiar with how the application works. By issuing a single command, you can add the contents of a page to a Microsoft Outlook message window that you address and send to others. You can also share a page in other formats, including as a PDF file, or attach a page to a message as a separate file. You can change settings in the OneNote Options dialog box to control how OneNote content is distributed in e-mail.

In addition to using e-mail to share OneNote content, you use e-mail to invite other people to collaborate on a shared notebook and to send a link to other users when you set up a notebook for sharing.

In the sections that follow, you'll learn how to share and manage the content in a OneNote notebook via e-mail.

E-Mailing Others About the Notebook

At the end of the process you follow to share a notebook in OneNote, you see a message box that informs you that anyone who has permission to access the location you specified (a network location or a Windows Live SkyDrive folder) can now work with the notebook. The message box also provides a command button you can use to send an e-mail message with a link to the notebook's location to people you want to share the notebook with.

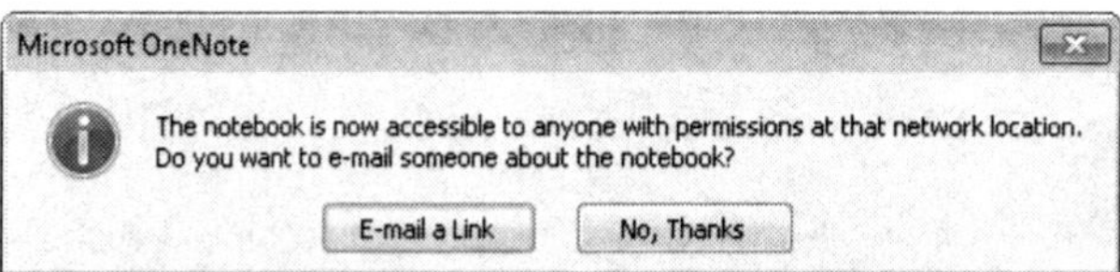

Use the E-Mail A Link button in this message box to let other users know the location of a shared notebook.

Click the E-Mail A Link button, and OneNote opens a message window in Outlook, complete with a subject line (which reads Invitation to OneNote Notebook: <name of notebook>) and a hyperlink that recipients can use to open the notebook in OneNote.

Of course, click No, Thanks in the message box if you need to perform other tasks before you notify other people where the notebook is located or aren't planning to share the notebook at all.

➤ To e-mail others about a notebook

1. Follow the steps in the section "Share OneNote Notebooks" to set up a shared notebook.
2. In the message box that OneNote displays after you click **Share Notebook**, click **E-Mail A Link**.
3. Address the e-mail message, and then click **Send**.

Inviting Others to View a Notebook

If you want to invite other people to share a notebook later—as an independent step instead of as a step in the process you follow to create or share a notebook—you can use the E-Mail Others About The Notebook link on the Share page in Backstage view. You can also click Invite People To This Notebook when you are working on the Info page, which takes you to the Share page.

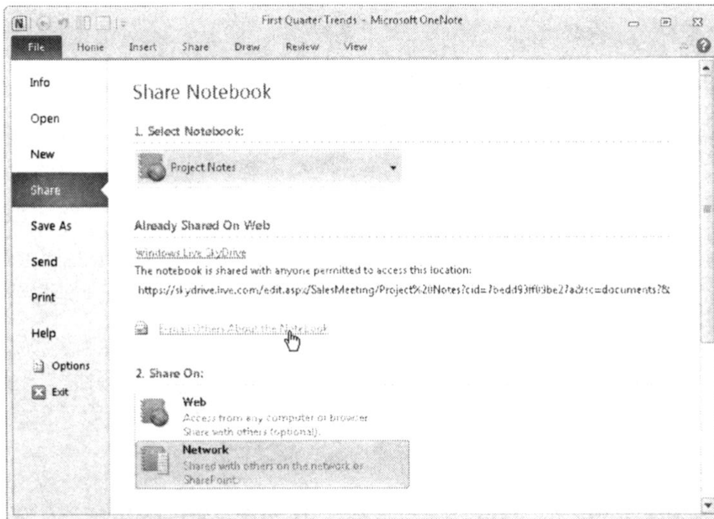

OneNote generates an e-mail message in Outlook when you click this link. Use the message to let other users know where a shared notebook is located.

Clicking the E-Mail Others About The Notebook link opens an Outlook message window with a link to the notebook. If you are working with a notebook you have stored in a Windows Live SkyDrive folder, the message will contain two links, one that opens the notebook in OneNote and the second that opens the notebook from Windows Live SkyDrive using a web browser.

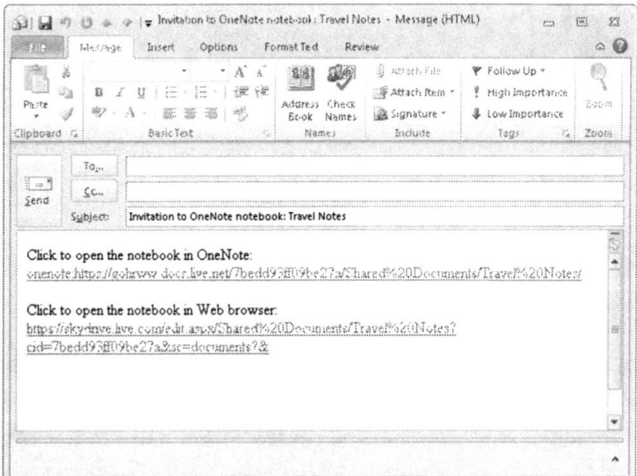

For a shared notebook stored on Windows Live SkyDrive, the invitation e-mail message that OneNote generates contains two links—one for OneNote and the other for opening the notebook in your browser.

➤ **To invite others to view a notebook**

1. On the ribbon, click **File**, and then click **Share**.
2. On the **Share** page, click **E-Mail Others About The Notebook**.
3. Address the e-mail message, and then click **Send**.

E-Mailing Pages in Shareable Formats

By using the E-Mail Page command in the E-Mail group on the Share tab (or in the Outlook group on the Home tab), you can send a OneNote page via e-mail to recipients you designate.

> **Tip You can also use the keyboard shortcut Ctrl+Shift+E to send the current page in e-mail.**

When you use the E-Mail Page command, OneNote adds the contents of the page, including the page title and the date and time stamp, to a message window in Outlook. OneNote inserts the page's name in the message window's Subject line. You need to add addresses for recipients, update the Subject line (if necessary), and then send the message. You can also edit the message's body as necessary.

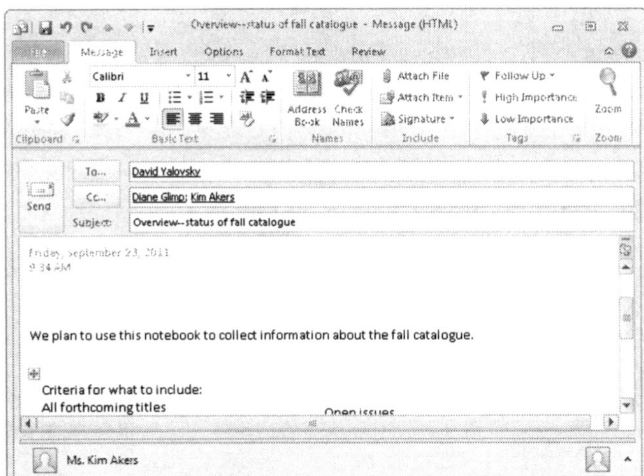

OneNote adds the contents of a page to an Outlook message window when you click E-Mail A Page. You need to insert addresses and add to the Subject line before sending the message.

You can find other options for sharing the content of a notebook on the Send page in Backstage view.

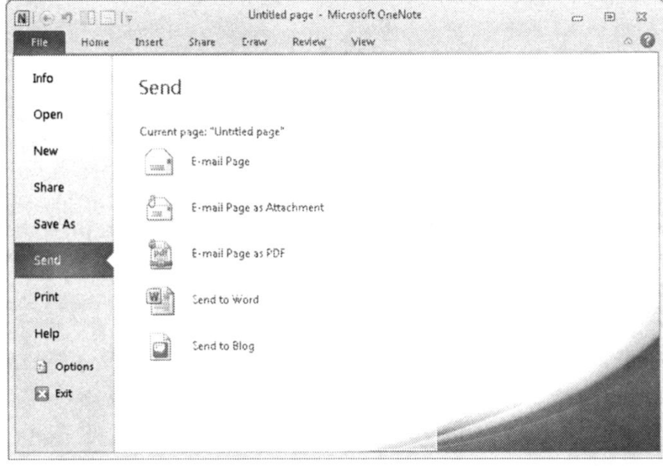

Choose one of the e-mail options on the Send page to share OneNote pages in formats such as PDF and MHTML.

This page lists three options for the format in which you can send a notebook page to recipients. The Send page also includes commands you can use to send a page to a Microsoft Word document (which you could distribute as an attachment) or to a blog post that you publish through Word:

- **E-Mail Page** This option produces the same result as when you click E-Mail Page on the Share tab or in the Outlook group on the Home tab. The content of the page appears in the message body. You need to complete the message by adding e-mail addresses for recipients and making any modifications to the subject line and message body.

- **E-Mail Page As Attachment** When you select this option, OneNote attaches the page to the message in two different formats. The page is attached in the .one format as a OneNote section and also in the .mht format, which lets recipients who don't have OneNote open the page in Internet Explorer, Microsoft Word, or the Word viewer application. (OneNote adds instructions about viewing the .mht file as a web page to the message's body.)

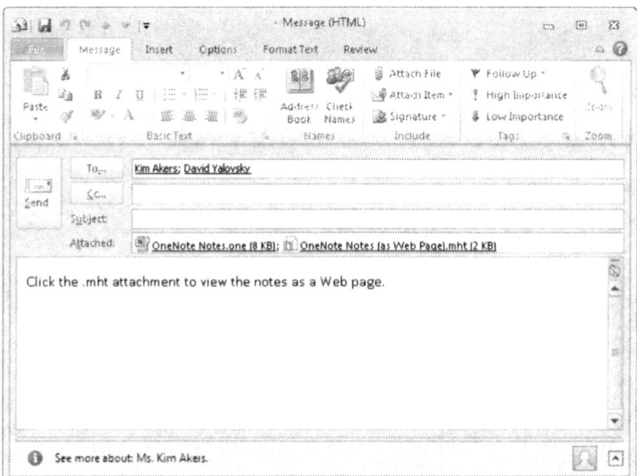

The E-Mail Page As Attachment option on the Send page attaches a OneNote file and an .mht file to a message. You can open an .mht file in Internet Explorer or Microsoft Word, but not all browsers support this format.

> **Important The .mht file name extension is associated with the MHTML format. (MHTML is an abbreviation for MIME HTML.) The page's contents, including text and images, are saved along with formatting in a single file. You cannot directly open MHTML files in browsers other than Internet Explorer or Opera, but you can install an add-on to work with .mht files in browsers such as Firefox or Safari.**

- **E-Mail Page As PDF** To attach the current page as a PDF file (the Portable Document Format used by Adobe Acrobat and related applications), use this option. OneNote displays a progress bar to show that the page is being converted to PDF and then displays an Outlook message window with the attachment in place and the name of the page inserted in the Subject line. The page name is also used for the file name, with "as PDF" added to identify the format. You can use the E-Mail Page As PDF option to distribute pages to people who don't have Microsoft Office installed, for example. Recipients do need at have Adobe Reader or another compatible application installed to open and read a PDF file.

The two other options on the Send page let you work with the content of a OneNote page in Word, either as a Word document or as the content of a blog post you create in Word. The option Send To Word inserts the content of a page in a Microsoft Word document. You can save the document to keep a record of the page, distribute the page via e-mail in Word format, or include the page in a longer document you are creating in Word. Choose the Send To Blog option to add the page's content to a document in Word and display the Blog Post tab on the Word ribbon. You can then publish the page—as it comes in from OneNote or after making edits and additions—to a blog by using the tools provided by Word.

➤ To e-mail OneNote pages in shareable formats

1. On the ribbon, click **File**, and then click **Send**.
2. On the **Send** page, select the option you want to use:
    - E-Mail Page
    - E-Mail Page As Attachment
    - E-Mail Page As PDF
3. Address the e-mail message in Outlook, and then click **Send**.

Configuring E-Mail Options in OneNote

The OneNote Options dialog box includes several settings for how OneNote works with e-mail. You'll find these settings on the Advanced page of the dialog box, in the area labeled E-Mail Sent From OneNote.

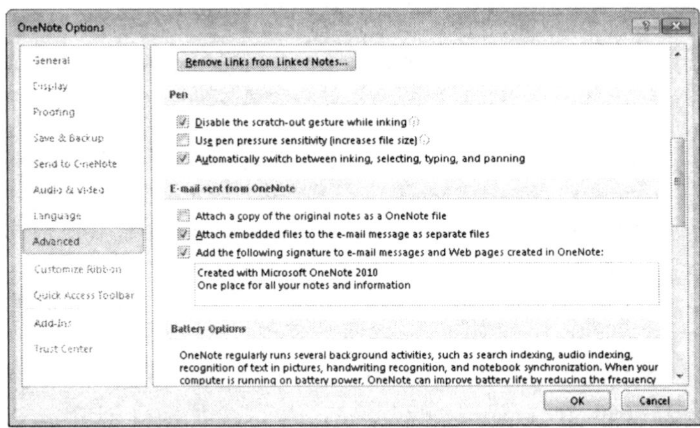

Use the OneNote Options dialog box to configure how OneNote handles attachments, embedded files, and e-mail signatures.

By default, OneNote inserts a page's content into the body of an e-mail message when you select E-Mail A Page (from the Outlook group on the Home tab or in the E-Mail group on the Share tab). Select the option Attach A Copy Of The Original Notes As A OneNote File if you want to also include the page as an attachment in the .one file format. If you select this option, recipients of the message can save the attachment and add the page to notebooks of their own.

The second option in this area, Attach Embedded Files To The E-Mail Message As Separate Files, is selected by default. With this setting, any files you have added to a page (by using the Attach File command on the Insert tab, for example) are included in the e-mail message as a separate attachment, and the body of the e-mail message displays the file's name as a placeholder.

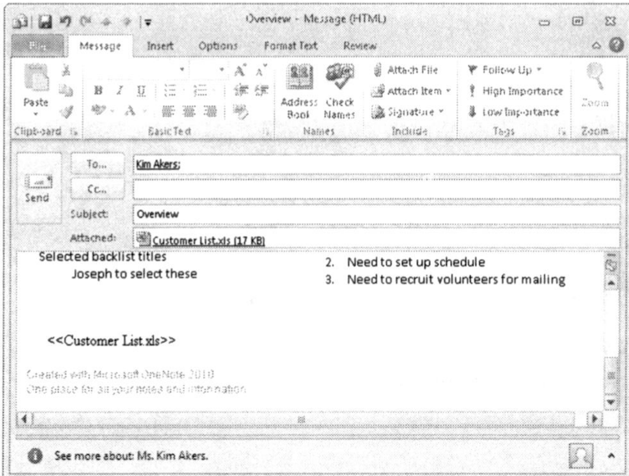

By default, OneNote attaches files embedded on a page as an attachment to an e-mail message. The page contains a placeholder.

If you clear this option, the embedded file is stripped from the page and not included as an attachment.

When you send a OneNote page via e-mail, OneNote by default adds a signature that reads "Created with Microsoft OneNote 2010 / One place for all your notes and information." You can change the signature that OneNote includes (or clear the option to include no signature at all). Change the text for the signature OneNote adds, or clear the option Add The Following Signature To E-Mail Messages And Web Pages Created In OneNote.

➤ To configure e-mail options in OneNote

1. On the ribbon, click **File**, and then click **Options**.
2. In the **OneNote Options** dialog box, click **Advanced**.

3. In the area **E-Mail Sent From OneNote**, select or clear the following options:
    - Attach A Copy Of The Original Notes As A OneNote File
    - Attach Embedded Files To The E-Mail Message As Separate Files
    - Add The Following Signature To E-Mail Messages And Web Pages Created In OneNote.
4. Modify or add to the text for the e-mail signature you want OneNote to insert.
5. Click **OK**.

Practice Tasks

The practice files for these tasks are located in the practice files folder for Microsoft OneNote 2010. You can save the results of these exercises in the same folder. Change the file name so that you don't overwrite the sample files. When you are done, try performing the following tasks:

- Open the notebook Fall Catalog Production.
- Use the Info page to invite another user to share this notebook.
- Work with several pages in this notebook by using the E-Mail Page command and the commands on the Send page in Backstage view to see how you can share OneNote content via e-mail.
- Configure e-mail options so that embedded files are not included in an e-mail message sent by OneNote.

2.3 Collaborate in OneNote

As you saw in the previous sections of this chapter, you frequently work with commands on the Share tab when you collaborate with others on a notebook. In this section, you'll learn about the commands on the Share tab that help you find notes by different authors, see recent changes to a notebook, hide author initials when you need to, and mark a note added by another of the notebook's users so that you know whether you have read it.

Marking Coauthor Edits as Read or Unread

When you open a shared notebook, notes added by other users since the last time you opened the notebook are highlighted. In addition, in the page tabs bar, OneNote displays the names of pages with unread notes in bold. You can use the commands in the Unread group on the Share tab to navigate to pages that contain unread notes and to mark notes as read or unread.

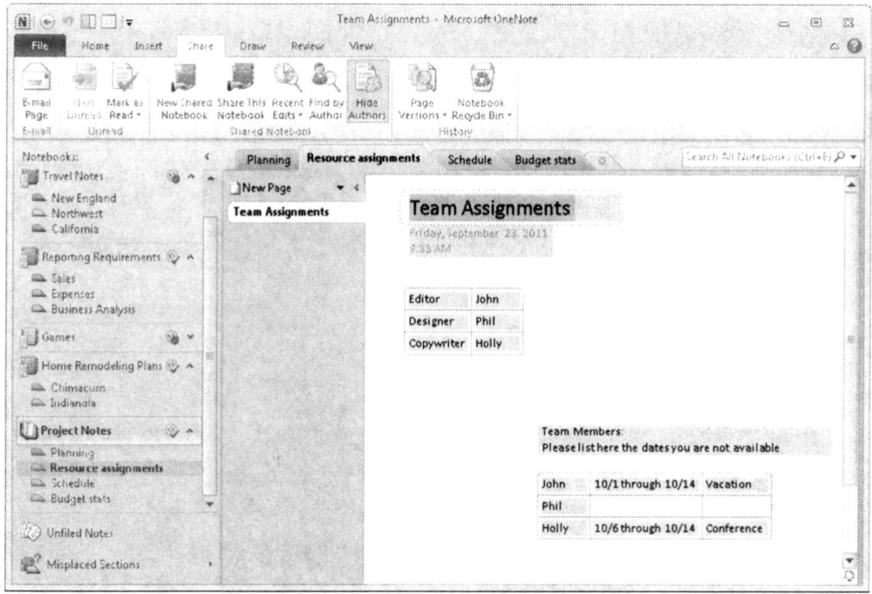

Unread notes are highlighted by default. Use the Mark As Read menu on the Share tab to manage the status of read and unread notes.

To move to the next page in a notebook with notes you haven't read, go to the Share tab and click the Next Unread button. Using the Mark As Read menu, you can do the following to indicate you've read notes entered by others since the last time you opened a notebook:

- Click Mark As Read (or press Ctrl+Q) to show you have read notes on a page. The notes on the page are no longer highlighted, and the page's name in the page tabs bar is no longer shown in bold. You can choose Mark As Unread (or press Ctrl+Q again) if you want to revert to showing the highlighting.
- Click Mark Notebook As Read to show you've read all new notes in a notebook.
- Clear the check mark for the option Show Unread Changes In This Notebook if you don't want to track the read/unread status of new notes.

➤ To review unread notes in a shared notebook

1. Click the **Share** tab.
2. In the **Unread** group, click **Next Unread** to move to the next page in the notebook that contains unread notes.
3. Use the commands on the **Mark As Read** menu to do the following:
   - Choose Mark As Read to indicate you have read notes.
   - Choose Mark As Unread to indicate you have not read the notes on a page.
   - Choose Mark Notebook As Read to indicate you have read all the notes in a notebook.
   - Clear the check mark for Show Unread Changes In This Notebook to turn off this feature. (Select the option again to show unread notes.)

Viewing Recent Edits

The Recent Edits menu, in the Shared Notebooks group on the Share tab, lets you choose an option for seeing the edits made to a notebook over a specific period of time. You can choose Today, for example, to see the most recent changes, or Since Yesterday to review any additions or changes made since the day before. You can also choose a period of time such as the last seven days or a span as long as the past six months. Choose the option All Pages Sorted By Date to see a list of pages organized by time period.

When you choose an option to view recent edits, OneNote opens that Search Results pane and lists sections and pages that match the option you selected.

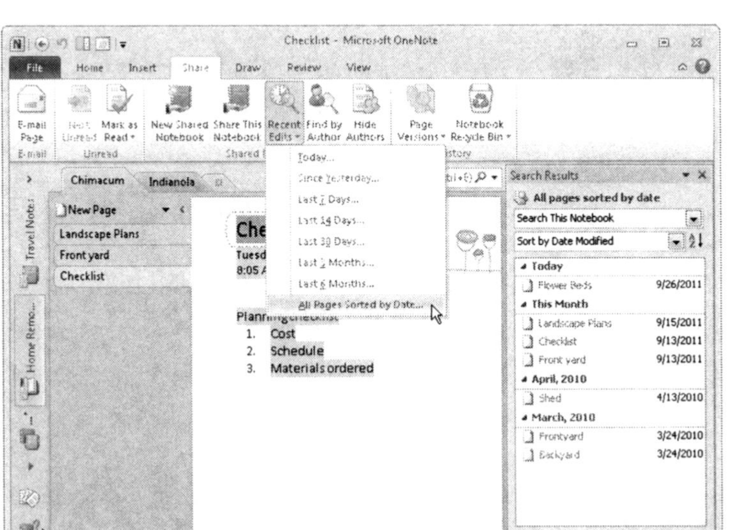

You can see the edits made to a notebook over a specific period of time. Change the search scope in the Search Results pane to view all notebooks, a section, or a page.

In the Search Results pane, the search scope is set to Search This Notebook. You can choose an alternative from the search scope list to search only the current section, search the current section group, or search all open notebooks. To switch to a different search scope by using the keyboard, press Ctrl+E, Tab, Space.

> **See Also** For detailed information about searching in OneNote, see "Search OneNote" in Chapter 3, "Organizing and Finding Notes."

Use the Sort button at the right of the Sort By list to change the order from ascending to descending. Choosing the Recent Edits command specifies that the Search Results pane is sorted by date modified. With the Search Results pane open, however, you can use the Sort By list to see results by section, title, and author, as well.

➤ To view recent edits

1. On the **Share** tab, click **Recent Edits**, and then select the time period you want to apply.
2. In the **Search Results** pane, click the page you want to review.
3. To change the search scope, select the scope you want to use from the search scope list at the top of the **Search Results** pane.

Finding Notes by Author

Another use of the Search Results pane is to let you find notes added or changed by a specific author. Click Find By Author in the Shared Notebook group to display the Search Results pane with the option Sort By Author selected in the list of sorting options.

You can expand and collapse the entries for a particular author by using the arrow to the left of an author's name. Click an entry in the list to jump to that page. Use the Sort button to sort the entries in ascending or descending order.

> **Tip** You can use the Search Results pane independently of the commands on the Shared Notebooks page. You can select a different sorting option, for example, or select a different search scope.

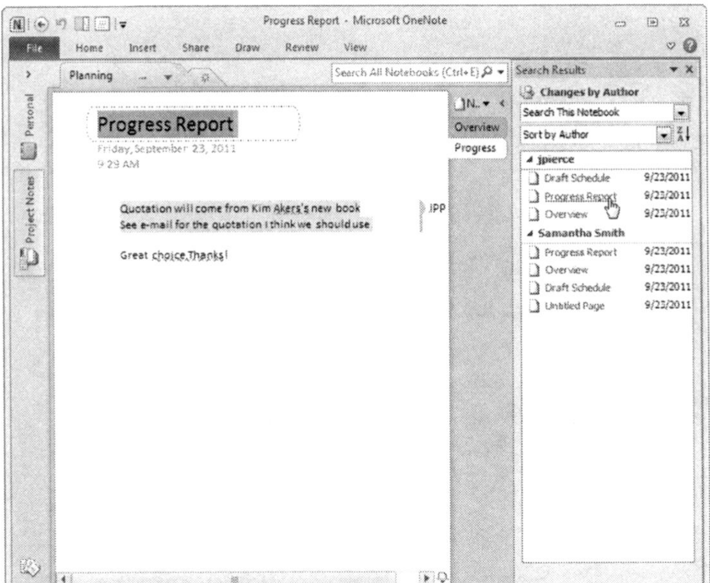

The Find By Author command organizes search results by author and by date.

➤ To search notes by author

1. On the **Share** tab, click **Find By Author**.
2. In the **Search Results** pane, expand the section for the author whose notes you want to search.
3. Click the page you want to review. Notes by that author are highlighted on the screen.
4. To change the search scope, open the search scope list or use the keyboard.

Hiding Author Initials

In a shared notebook, OneNote identifies the person who inserted or edited a note by displaying that person's initials next to the note. You can see more details—the person's full name and the last modified date and time—by pointing to the initials to reveal a ScreenTip.

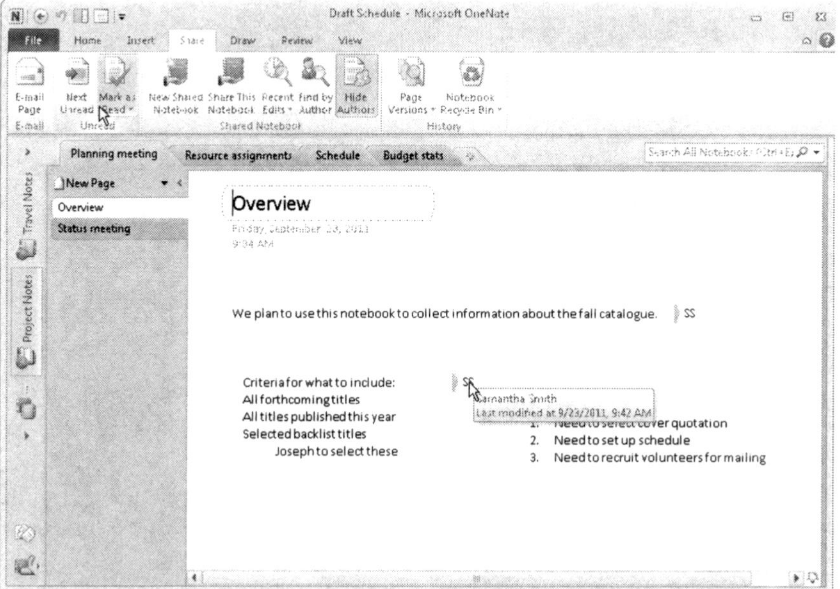

Notes added by other users are identified by their initials. You can see more details in a ScreenTip. Click Hide Authors if you don't need to see this information.

If you want to see the page without the identifying initials, click Hide Authors in the Shared Notebook group on the Share tab. To reveal the initials again, click Hide Authors a second time. OneNote doesn't display initials next to the notes or other content that you add yourself.

Changing Your Identity

You can change the initials that OneNote (and other Office programs) use to identify you by opening the OneNote Options dialog box and changing the initials under Personalize Your Copy Of Microsoft Office. You might consider changing your personal initials to a department abbreviation (for example, Sales or Ops) if you are working on a notebook in your role as a department representative rather than individually. Keep in mind, however, that the characters you type in the Initials box are used to identify you not only for OneNote notes, but also for features such as comments and revisions in Word. Revert to the initials you want to use by default after you make a change for a specific purpose. Also, a change you make doesn't ripple back to notes you entered previously. If Samantha Smith changes SS to Sales, OneNote still uses SS to identify notes that she created when those initials were entered in the Initials box. Sales is used for notes added after the change and since the notebook was synchronized.

➤ **To display or hide author initials**

→ On the **Share** tab, click **Hide Authors**.

Practice Tasks

The practice files for these tasks are located in the practice files folder for Microsoft OneNote 2010. You can save the results of these exercises in the same folder. Change the file name so that you don't overwrite the sample files. When you are done, try performing the following tasks:

- Open the notebook Project Notes, and then create several notes on the pages the notebook contains.
- Use the commands on the Share tab to locate any unread notes.
- Use the Recent Edits and Find By Author commands to search for notes inserted at a specific time and by specific authors.

Objective Review

Before finishing this chapter, be sure you have mastered the following skills:

- Share OneNote notebooks
- Share OneNote content via e-mail
- Collaborate in OneNote

3 Organizing and Finding Notes

The skills tested in this section of the Microsoft Office Specialist exam for Microsoft OneNote 2010 are related to organizing and finding notes. Specifically, the following objectives are associated with this set of skills:

3.1 Use OneNote notebook organizational tools

3.2 Search OneNote

3.3 Use history and backups in OneNote

3.4 Use the Save As command

3.5 Use quick filing

3.6 Use and manage tags

Throughout this chapter, you'll see examples of the features you can use to organize and find notes in OneNote notebooks. These capabilities include options for implementing the structure of a notebook—adding sections to section groups and subpages to pages when you need a detailed level of organization. You'll also learn about how you conduct searches, view previous versions of a page, and work with the built-in recycle bin OneNote includes with each notebook. In addition, you'll see how to save pages and notebooks in different formats, how to configure settings for where content from other applications ends up in OneNote, and how to apply and manage tags, which are a device you use to identify different types of notes.

3.1 Use OneNote Notebook Organizational Tools

Like conventional loose-leaf notebooks, OneNote notebooks are organized by sections, with each section containing one or more pages. No specific restriction applies to the number of sections you can define in a notebook—and when the number of sections increases, you can organize sections into section groups. Similarly, you can define subpages as child pages you associate with a parent page.

Other organizational tools are available as well, including the ability to merge sections, using color coding to identify notebooks and sections, and creating side notes, which let you jot down an idea as you work that you can later incorporate into a notebook.

Merging Sections

When you want to combine the notes and content stored in separate sections, you can merge one section with the other. The sections can be in the same notebook or in different notebooks. After OneNote merges two sections, it prompts you to delete the original section. Choose this option if you don't need a separate copy of what are now duplicate notes.

To start merging sections, choose Merge Into Another Section from the menu that appears when you right-click a section name in the Navigation bar or the section's tab. In the Merge Section dialog box, select the section you want to merge with the first section or type the section's name in the search box at the top of the dialog box to locate the section you want. The search option is especially useful when you have a large number of notebooks to scroll through.

> **Tip** OneNote filters the list of sections displayed in the Merge Section dialog box as you type each character of a section's title.

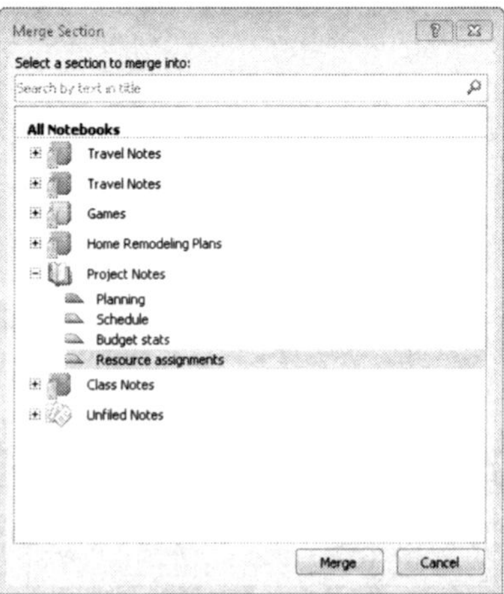

In the Merge Section dialog box, select the section you want to merge another with or use the search box to locate that section.

When you click Merge, OneNote displays a message box in which you confirm the action. Note the warning that you cannot undo the merge. If you want to proceed, click Merge Sections. OneNote then displays another message box that tells you that the sections were merged successfully. Click Delete here if you want OneNote to remove the original section from its notebook.

> **Tip** You might want to rename the combined section to be sure the name now describes the merged content. Right-click the section name in the Navigation bar and choose Rename from the menu.

➤ **To merge sections**

1. In the Navigation bar, right-click the section you want to merge with another, and then choose **Merge Into Another Section**.
2. In the **Merge Section** dialog box, select the section you want to merge with the first (or use the search box to locate the section).
3. Click **Merge**.
4. In the OneNote message box, click **Merge Sections** to confirm the operation.
5. In the next message box, click **Delete** if you want OneNote to delete the original section.

Creating a Section Group

To help consolidate the sections in a notebook in which you have defined a large number of sections, you can create section groups. When you need even more detailed organization, you can nest a section group within another section group.

Like sections, section groups appear on the Navigation bar and with the section tabs at the top of the page. You can expand and collapse section groups in the Navigation bar to view or hide the sections they contain, and you can drag section groups in the Navigation bar to change the order in which they appear in a notebook.

> **Tip** Notebook sections that are not included in a section group always appear before section groups on the Navigation bar.

To create a section group, right-click the notebook name in the Navigation bar and then click New Section Group. Name the section group, and then add sections by dragging sections to it or by creating new sections for the group.

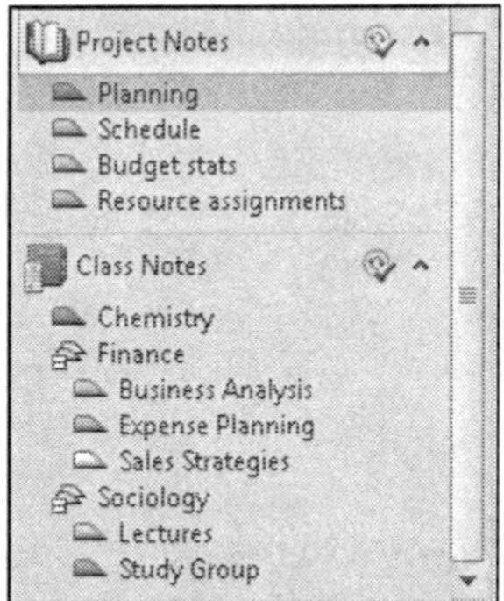

Create section groups when you need to organize a large number of sections in a notebook.

How OneNote Stores Section Groups

If you look at the folder structure for a OneNote notebook (by opening the default location where notebooks are stored, for example), you'll see that section groups are subfolders within the folder that contains the notebook. The subfolder for the section group contains OneNote section files (with the .one file name extension).

➤ To create a section group

1. Right-click a notebook in the Navigation bar, and then choose **New Section Group**.
2. Type a name for the group.
3. Create new sections for the section group, or, on the Navigation bar, drag sections you've already defined into the new section group.

Color-Coding Notebooks and Sections

To help identify and organize notebooks, you can apply a specific color to notebook icons that appear on the Navigation bar and also to notebook sections. The color you select for a section is used as a background on the section tab and in the color band that OneNote displays along the left of each page in a section.

To assign the color you want to use for a notebook, right-click the notebook in the Navigation bar and then choose Properties. In the Notebook Properties dialog box, pick a color from the palette that appears when you click the down arrow beside the Color button. You can choose from a group of 16 colors.

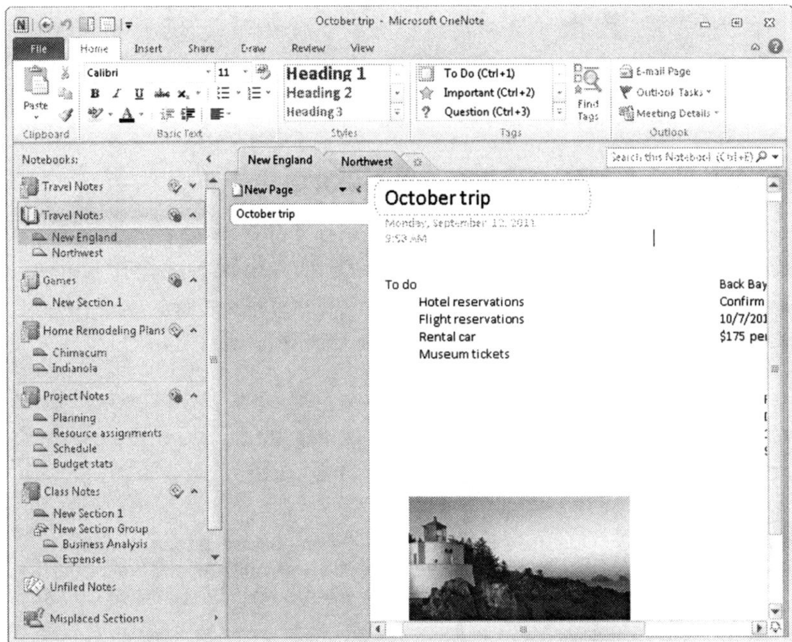

The color you assign to a notebook appears on the Navigation bar icon. The color you assign to a section appears on the section tab and in a band down the left side of the page.

> **See Also** For more information about using the Notebook Properties dialog box, see "Configuring Notebook Settings and Properties" in Chapter 1, "Managing the OneNote Environment."

You can assign a color to a section by right-clicking a section in the Navigation bar or clicking the section tab at the top of the notebook window and then choosing Section Color. Here, too, you can choose from 16 colors or choose None to not apply a color to this section.

➤ To color-code notebooks

1. In the Navigation bar, right-click the notebook and choose **Properties**.
2. In the **Notebook Properties** dialog box, click the **Color** button and choose the color you want to apply.

➤ To color-code sections

➜ In the Navigation bar, right-click the section, click **Section Color**, and then choose the color you want to apply.

Protecting Sections with a Password

If you use a section of a shared notebook to record and store personal or confidential information, you can apply a password to the section to control who can work with it. (If you want to assign a password to each section of a notebook, you need to do that in separate steps; you can't assign a password to the notebook itself.)

To define a password and set options for how a section is protected, you use the Password Protection pane, which OneNote displays when you right-click a section in the Navigation bar and choose Password Protect This Section.

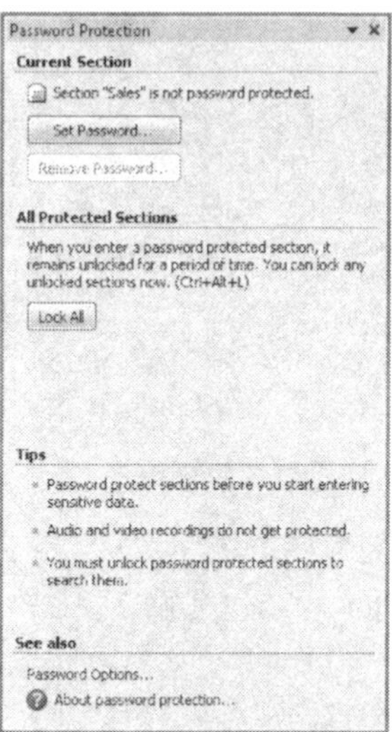

Use this task pane to define a password for a section. Sections stay open as you work on them and are locked after a period of time you can set in the OneNote Options dialog box.

The Set Password button opens the Password Protection dialog box, which provides a text box in which you define the password and another you use to confirm it.

> **Tip** As the Password Protection dialog box warns you, you should be sure not to lose or forget the password. The password can't be recovered, and you will lose your data.

After you define a password, OneNote replaces the Set Password button with the Change Password button and enables the Remove Password button. Of course, you need to know the section's password to change it or to remove it.

After you define a section password, OneNote keeps the section unlocked as long as you work in it and then locks the section after the time period specified in the OneNote Options dialog box. To lock the section (so that the password is required to gain access to it), click Lock All in the Password Protection pane.

When you display a section that is protected with a password, OneNote indicates that the section is protected and instructs you to click the notice or press Enter to unlock the section. Enter the password to gain access to that section.

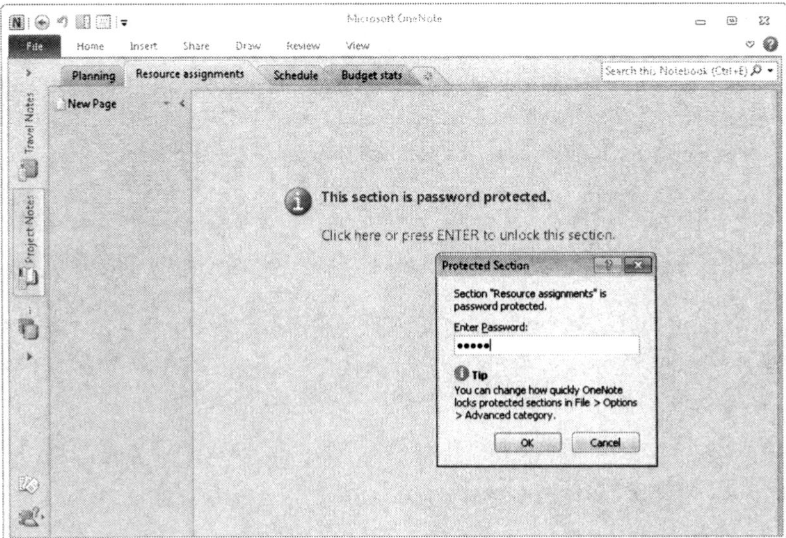

You'll see a notification like this when you enter a protected section that is locked. Enter the password to unlock the section.

OneNote keeps a protected section unlocked for a specific period of time, which you can configure in the OneNote Options dialog box. Click Password Options in the Password Protection pane to display the Advanced page of the dialog box, and then scroll to the Passwords area. Two of the three settings in this area are selected by default. Adjust the time period after which OneNote locks a protected section. You can choose one of the intervals (between 1 minute and 1 day) that OneNote defines. You can also select the option by which OneNote locks sections immediately after you move to a different section. The third option in this group deals with add-in programs. The option enables add-ins to use protected sections when they are unlocked.

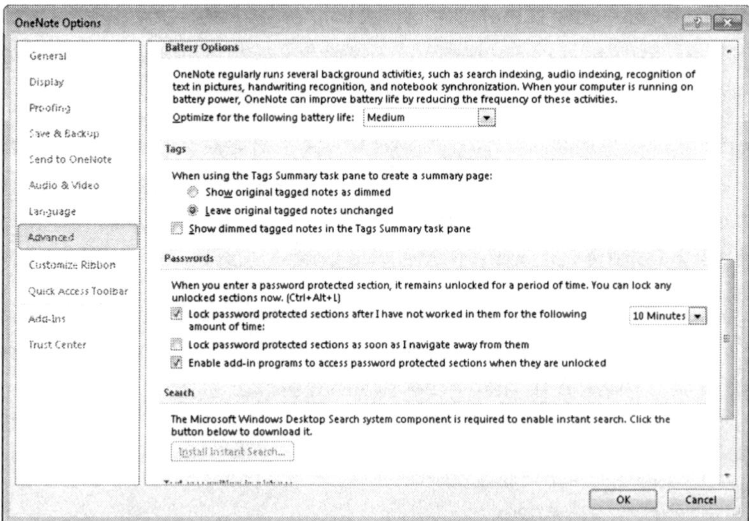

Tip The contents of password-protected sections are not searched unless they are unlocked.

➤ To protect a section with a password

1. In the Navigation bar, right-click the section and choose **Password Protect This Section**.
2. In the **Password Protection** pane, click **Set Password**.
3. In the **Password Protection** dialog box, type the password you want to use and then type the password again to confirm it.

➤ To change a password for a password-protected section

1. In the Navigation bar, right-click the section and choose **Password Protect This Section**.
2. In the **Password Protection** pane, click **Change Password**.
3. In the **Change Password** dialog box, type the current password. Type the new password, and then type the new password again to confirm it.

➤ To remove a password

1. In the Navigation bar, right-click the section and choose **Password Protect This Section**.
2. In the **Password Protection** pane, click **Remove Password**.
3. In the **Remove Password** dialog box, type the current password and then click **OK**.

➤ To configure password options

1. In the **Password Protection** pane, click **Password Options**.

   You can also click **File, Options**, and then click **Advanced** in the **OneNote Options** dialog box.

2. Scroll to the **Passwords** area of the **OneNote Options** dialog box.

3. Set the time interval after which OneNote locks protected sections. Clear or set other options as they apply to your use of OneNote.

Grouping and Collapsing Subpages

You can create a subpage to add another level of organization to the structure of a notebook. You can nest subpages two levels below a main page.

To specify a page as a subpage, right-click the page in the page tabs bar and choose Make Subpage. Also, when you point to an existing subpage and then click the New Page icon that floats beside the page tabs bar, that action creates a subpage. The keyboard alternative for creating a subpage below the current page is to press Ctrl+Alt+Shift+N.

> **Tip** If you want to designate a group of pages as subpages, hold down the Ctrl key, select each page, and then right-click the group and choose Make Subpage.

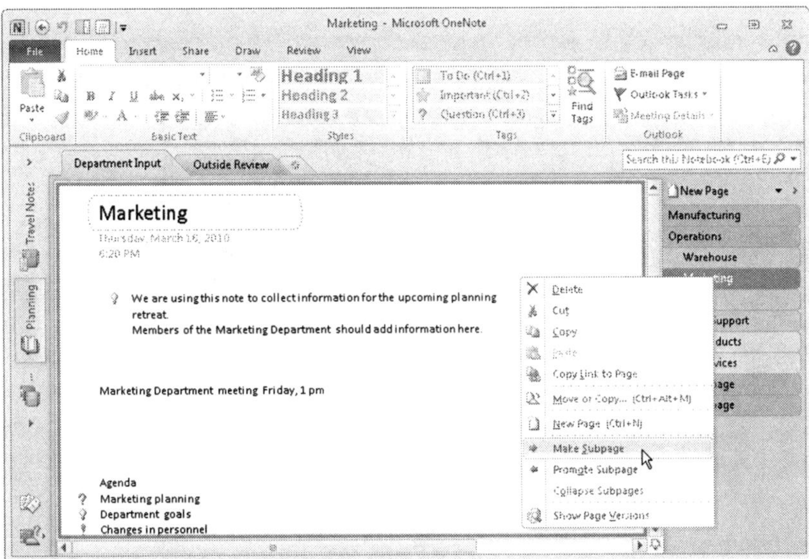

Subpages add another level of detail to the structure of a notebook. Use the menu shown here to create, promote, and collapse (or expand) subpages.

You can use a variety of menu commands and keyboard combinations to control whether subpages appear in the page tabs bar and to determine their level in the structure of a notebook. To hide subpages, right-click a subpage and choose Collapse Subpages. To display subpages, right-click the main page and choose Expand Subpages. Use the Promote Subpage command on the shortcut menu to make a subpage a main page (or to promote a subpage's subpage to the current level). You can use the keyboard combinations Ctrl+Alt+] and Ctrl+Alt+[to increase or decrease the indent level of the current page, or simply drag a page left or right to change its level of indentation.

➤ **To create a subpage**

➜ In the page tabs bar, right-click a page and choose **Make Subpage**.

➤ **To collapse subpages**

➜ In the page tabs bar, right-click a subpage and choose **Collapse Subpages**.

➤ **To expand subpages**

➜ In the page tabs bar, right-click a subpage and choose **Expand Subpages**.

➤ **To promote a subpage**

➜ In the page tabs bar, right-click a subpage and choose **Promote Subpage**.

Using Side Notes

Side notes enable you to record an idea—even make a quick sketch—without having OneNote open (although you can also create side notes from OneNote when it is running). You record a side note in a OneNote window that provides a subset of commands from the regular ribbon and does not display Navigation bar or page tabs.

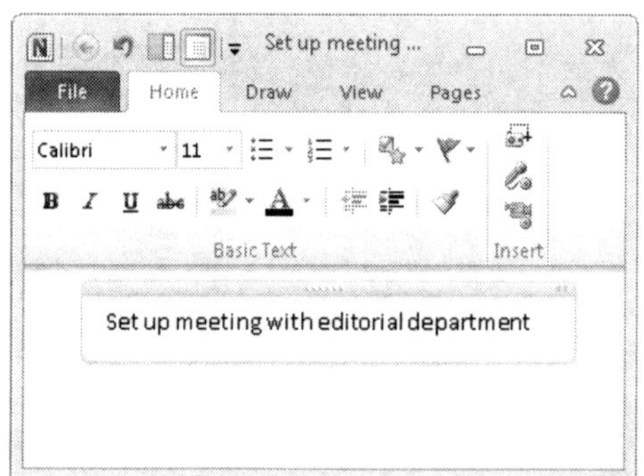

The side note window opens when you press the Windows logo key+N. Click the heart-shaped icon at the right side of the window to work with the commands on the ribbon.

When you set up OneNote, a OneNote icon is displayed by default in the notification area of the Windows taskbar. The default action that occurs when you click the icon is to open a side note window. You can also open a side note window by pressing the Windows logo key+N.

> **Tip** If you want to keep the side note window open and display it on top of other windows, click Keep On Top on the View tab of the side note window.

> **See Also** For information about setting options for the OneNote icon, see "Configuring Display Settings" in Chapter 1.

OneNote sends side notes to the Unfiled Notes section, which appears at the bottom of the Navigation bar. You can display unfiled notes and then drag the pages to the notebooks they relate to or create a notebook to house them.

When you are working in OneNote, you can display a side note window by clicking New Side Note on the ribbon's View tab.

➤ To create a side note

➜ With the OneNote icon displayed in the Windows taskbar, press Windows logo key+N, or click the icon.

Practice Tasks

The practice files for these tasks are located in the practice files folder for Microsoft OneNote 2010. You can save the results of these exercises in the same folder. Change the file name so that you don't overwrite the sample files. When you are done, try performing the following tasks:

- Open the notebook Budget Planning (or use one of your own notebooks and adapt the following steps).
- Merge the Marketing section with the Sales section. Rename the group so that it reflects the combined sections.
- Create a section group named Operations Departments, and then add the Manufacturing and Finance sections to that section group.
- Assign a different color to the Division Goals section and to the notebook.
- Define a password for the Marketing and Sales section. Lock that section, and then open it by providing the password.
- Create a page in the Marketing and Sales section named Revenue Plan. Create subpages of this page for each quarter (Quarter 1 through Quarter 4).
- Practice creating and adding side notes to this notebook.

3.2 Search OneNote

In OneNote, you can search on a page, within a section or a section group, within the current notebook, or in all open notebooks. OneNote's search feature instantly filters results as you type information in the search box. If you want to work with results in a separate task pane, you can display the Search Results pane, where you can sort results by date or title, for example, and also change the scope of your search.

Searching Notebooks, Sections, and Pages

To search for a word or phrase on the current page, press Ctrl+F to activate the search box. Type the word you are looking for, and OneNote highlights each instance of the word. To the left of the search box, OneNote shows how many instances of the term appear on the page. Move from the first instance to the next (and back) by using the arrows, or use F3 and Shift+F3 to move through the page.

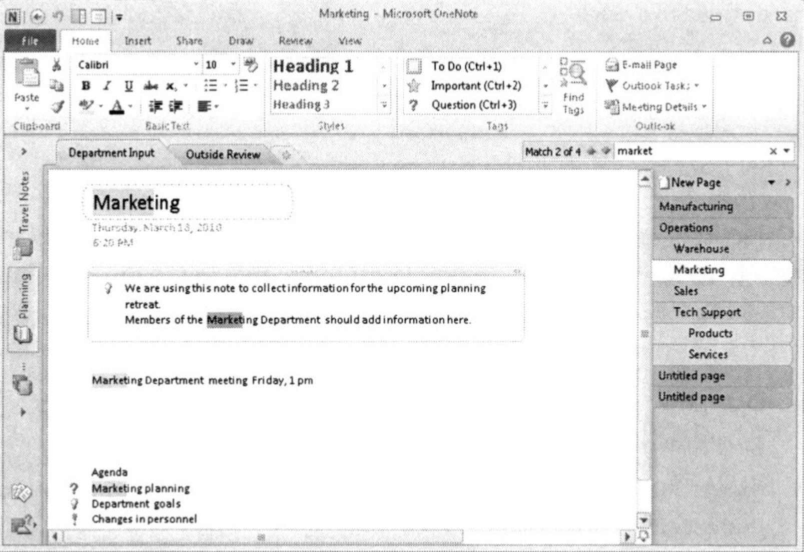

Press Ctrl+F to start searching for a term on the current page. Use the Match list beside the search box to move to the next or previous instance of the term.

> **Tip** You can use the AND and OR operators (use the uppercase characters) to perform more complex searches. Use quotation marks around a term to restrict the results to a specific phrase.

When you want to find a note beyond the current page, press Ctrl+E to make the search box active. OneNote displays a list of open notebooks, and as you enter the text you want to locate, OneNote quickly filters the contents of the list to show you relevant notes.

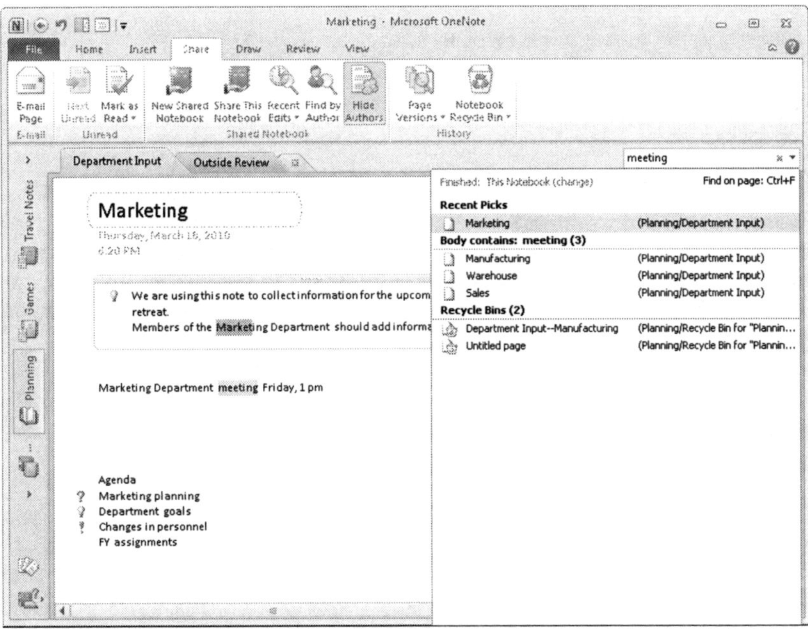

Press Ctrl+E to expand a search to the current notebook. Results are shown in a list that OneNote filters as you type the text you are searching for.

If you want to change the search scope, click the arrow at the right side of the search box and choose one of the options: This Section, This Section Group, This Notebook, All Notebooks. You can choose Set This Scope As The Default at the bottom of the menu to specify the current scope as the one you want OneNote to use each time you start a search.

OneNote provides a group of keyboard shortcuts you can use to conduct searches and move through results, summarized in the following table:

To do this	Press
Move the insertion point to the search box to search all notebooks.	Ctrl+E
While searching all notebooks, preview the next result.	Down Arrow
While searching all notebooks, go to the selected result and dismiss search.	Enter

To do this	Press
Change the search scope.	Ctrl+E, Tab, Space
Open the Search Results pane.	Alt+O after searching
Search only the current page.	Ctrl+F
While searching the current page, move to the next result.	Enter or F3
While searching the current page, move to the previous result.	Shift+F3
Dismiss search and return to the page.	Esc

Important If you are using a computer that runs Microsoft Windows XP, you might need to install the Windows Desktop Search component to search OneNote most effectively. Click File, Options in OneNote, and then click the Install Instant Search button on the Advanced page of the OneNote Options dialog box.

➤ To search notebooks, sections, and pages

1. Press Ctrl+F to activate the search box and search for text on the current page.
2. Press Ctrl+E to switch to searching all notebooks.
3. To change the search scope, click the arrow at the right side of the search box, and then choose an option for the search scope you want to use.

Displaying the Search Results Pane

Instead of working in the results list, you can open the Search Results pane by clicking the link at the bottom of the results list or by pressing Alt+O. In this pane, search results are initially sorted by the date modified. You can also sort by section or by title, and you can use the sort order button to arrange results in ascending or descending order.

See Also You also use the Search Results pane to locate recent edits and notes by specific authors in a shared notebook. For more information, see "Viewing Recent Edits" and "Finding Notes by Author" in Chapter 2, "Sharing and Collaborating."

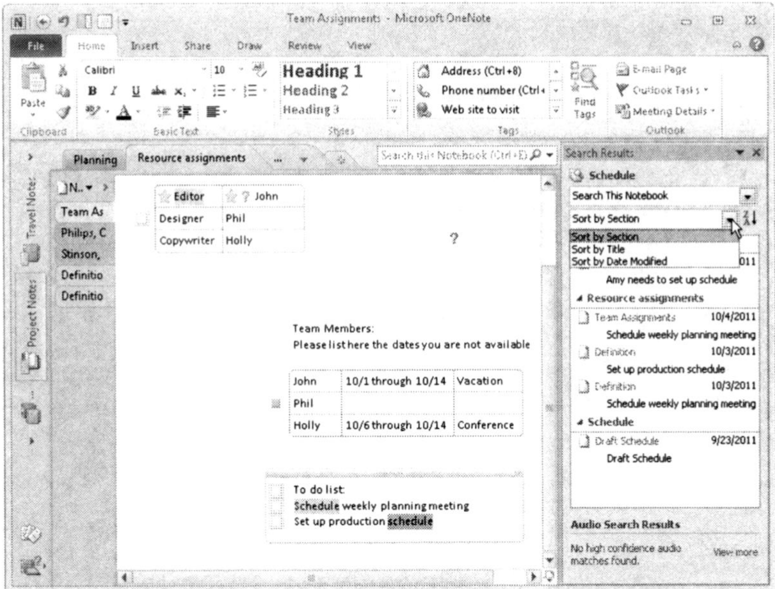

Press Alt+O after you conduct a search to open the Search Results pane. Here, you can sort search results by title, date, or section; change the sort order; and change the search scope.

By default, the Search Results pane shows search results for the current notebook. To change the scope of the results shown in the Search Results pane, open the list at the top of the pane, and choose Search This Section, Search This Section Group, or Search All Notebooks.

The Search pane updates results immediately when you make a change to the search scope or the sorting arrangement.

➤ To work with the Search Results pane

1. Press Ctrl+E to active the search box. Start a search to view the results. Press Alt+O or click the link at the bottom of the results list to open the **Search Results** pane.
2. Use the sort list to sort results by section, title, or date modified.
3. Click the sort button to sort results in ascending or descending order.
4. Use the search scope list to change the search scope from all notebooks to the current section, the current section group, or the current notebook.

Practice Tasks

The practice files for these tasks are located in the practice files folder for Microsoft OneNote 2010. You can save the results of these exercises in the same folder. Change the file name so that you don't overwrite the sample files. When you are done, try performing the following tasks:

- Open the notebook Department Meetings 2011.
- Display the page for March, and then search that page for the term "forecast".
- Switch to searching the full notebook, and search for the term "Marketing". Change the search scope to the current section and see how the results change.
- Open the Search Results pane, and sort the results by title.

3.3 Use History and Backups in OneNote

OneNote provides several features you can use to view and recover content from pages and notebooks that have changed or been deleted. Page versions show you earlier versions of a page and tell you who changed the page and when. You can also open backup copies that OneNote makes of notebooks and restore pages and sections, and you can recover material from OneNote's built-in recycle bin.

Working with Page Versions

OneNote maintains earlier versions of a page that has been changed by more than one user. To view these versions, display the Share tab, click the Page Versions button in the History group, and then choose Page Versions. An entry for each previous version, labeled with the modification date, is added to the page tabs bar.

Other options on the Page Versions menu let you delete all previous versions in the current section, section group, or notebook. You can also select the option Disable History For This Notebook if you have a reason that you don't want OneNote to track previous versions.

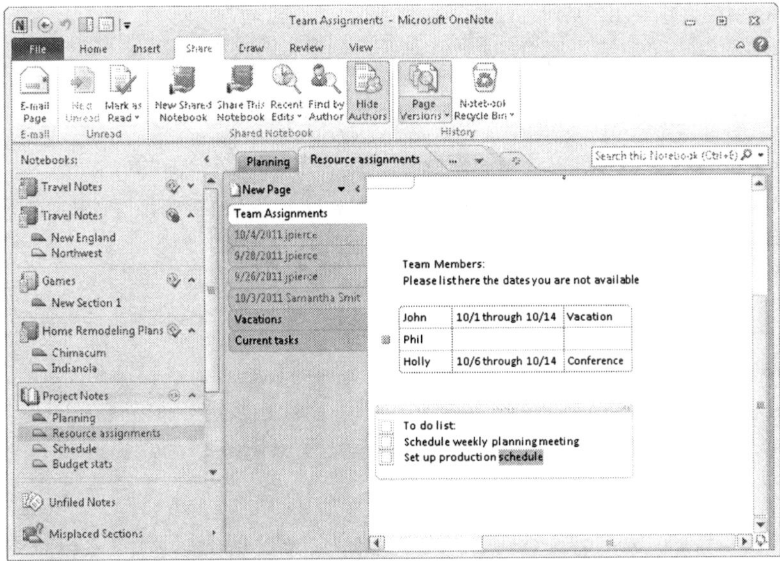

Earlier versions of a page are displayed in the page tabs bar. To restore a previous version, right-click the entry for that page and choose Restore Version.

When you click a previous version in the page tabs bar, OneNote displays a notification that indicates that the page is a previous version, that it will be deleted over time, and that you can click the notification if you want to restore that version to the notebook. The menu that appears when you click the notification includes the options available on the Page Versions menu and also provides options for deleting that version, copying the earlier version to another location in OneNote, and hiding the list of earlier versions.

➤ To view page versions

1. Select the page you want to work with.
2. On the **Share** tab, in the **History** group, click **Page Versions**.

➤ To delete page versions from a section or a notebook

1. On the **Share** tab, click the arrow next to **Page Versions**.
2. From the menu, select an option to delete page versions from the section, from the section group, or from the notebook.

➤ To manage a previous version

1. Right-click the earlier version in the page tabs bar.
2. Click **Restore Version** to add this version to the notebook.
3. Click **Delete Version** to delete this earlier version of the page.
4. Click **Copy Page To** to create a copy of the earlier version in a different section or notebook.

Using the Notebook Recycle Bin

Each notebook includes a built-in recycle bin where pages and sections are stored when you delete them. OneNote preserves content in the recycle bin for 60 days. The content in the recycle bin is read-only. You can't edit notes or insert new content when you view pages in the recycle bin.

To view the recycle bin, right-click a notebook in the Navigation bar and choose Notebook Recycle Bin. You can also click this command in the History group on the Share tab. To restore a page or section, right-click the item in the recycle bin and choose Move Or Copy. In the Move Or Copy dialog box, select the location where you want to place it—in the current notebook or in a different one.

You can empty the recycle bin by clicking this command on the Notebook Recycle Bin menu on the Share tab. If you choose the command Disable History For This Notebook, OneNote displays a message box that prompts you to confirm whether you want to delete page versions and empty the recycle bin.

➤ To work with a notebook's recycle bin

1. In the Navigation bar, right-click the notebook and choose **Notebook Recycle Bin**.
2. Right-click a section or a page you want to restore, and then click **Move Or Copy**.
3. In the **Move Or Copy** dialog box, select the location where you want to place the page or section you are restoring.

Opening Backup Notebooks

OneNote maintains backup copies of your notebooks, which it stores in a hidden folder in your user profile. When you need to refer to a backup, click File and then click Open Backups on the Info tab in Backstage view.

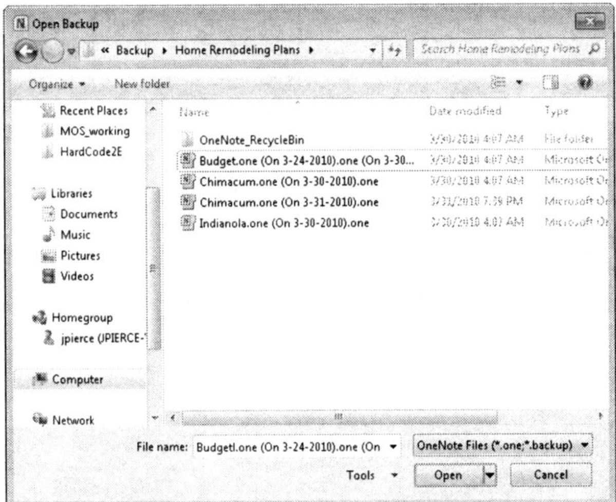

In the Open Backup dialog box, notebooks are organized in folders. Within each folder, you can see the backed-up section files with the date the backup was made. Double-click a backup file to open a read-only copy of the page or section in OneNote. The page does not appear in the current notebook. Instead, it is included under Open Sections, an entry that OneNote adds to the Navigation bar. From the Open Sections area, you can drag sections to any open notebook or right-click a section tab or a page tab and use the Move Or Copy command to add the backed-up page to a notebook.

You control backup settings in the OneNote Options dialog box, on the Save & Backup page. You can clear the option to have OneNote make backups automatically—which means you run more of a risk of losing data—and also set the time period for when OneNote makes backups. The intervals range from 1 minute to 6 weeks. (All notebooks are affected by these settings.) Click the Backup Changed Files Now or Backup All Notebooks Now button to create backup copies you can refer to later when you need to.

➤ To open a notebook backup

1. On the ribbon, click **File**. On the **Info** page, click **Open Backups**.
2. In the **Open Backups** dialog box, select the folder for the notebook you want to review and then click **Open**.
3. Select the section file you want to open, and then click **Open** again.
4. In the **Open Sections** area of the Navigation bar, right-click on the section you want to restore, choose **Move Or Copy**, and then use the **Move Or Copy Section** dialog box to select the location where you want to restore the backed-up section file.

Practice Tasks

No practice files are provided for the practice tasks in this section. Use your own notebooks to practice the skills described:

- Open a notebook you share with another user (if one is available).
- Display page versions.
- Open the recycle bin for the notebook.
- Open the backup for the notebook.

3.4 Use the Save As Command

In Chapters 1 and 2, you learned about several of the commands OneNote provides in Backstage view. In the following sections, you'll learn about the operations you can perform by using the Save As command.

The Save page is organized in two areas: Save Current and Select Format. In the first list, you select the object you want to save—the current page, the current section, or the complete notebook. In the Select Format section, the choices depend on the object you select. The following sections provide details about saving the current page and saving a notebook. The options for saving the current section are the same as for saving a page.

Saving the Current Page

You can choose from among seven file formats when you save the current page. The choices include the OneNote file format (.one) that is compatible with OneNote 2007 or the version used in OneNote 2010. Use the OneNote 2007 section format when you want to use the page in the earlier version of the program or make the page available to other users who work with OneNote 2007.

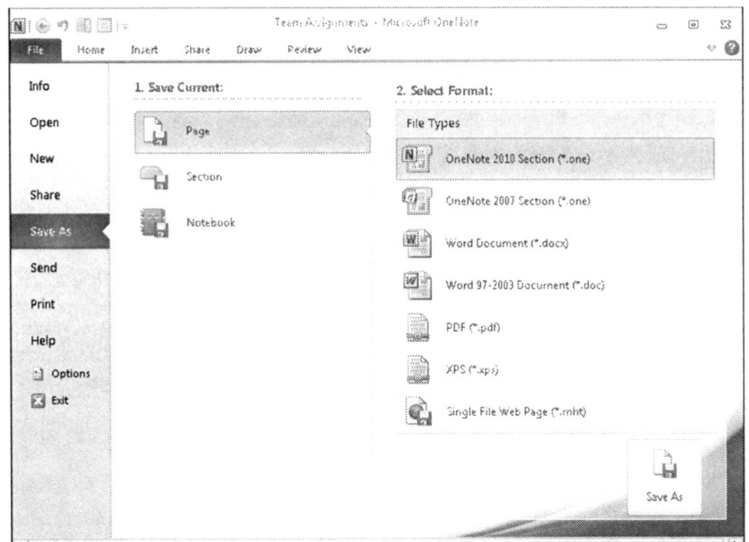

You can save the current page or the current section in seven formats. Use the OneNote 2007 Section option if you want to share a page with someone using an earlier version of the program.

The other choices of formats are as follows:

- **Word Document (*.docx)** The format for the XML-based standard supported by Word 2007 and Word 2010.
- **Word 97-2003 Document (*.doc)** The file format supported by versions of Microsoft Word prior to Word 2007.
- **PDF (*.pdf)** The Portable Document Format associated with Adobe Reader and Adobe Acrobat. You can save a page in this format if you need to make it available to someone who does not have Microsoft Office installed, for example.
- **XPS (*.xps)** The XML Paper Specification format defined by Microsoft. You can open .xps files in web browsers or in the XPS Viewer available from Microsoft.
- **Single File Web Page (*.mht)** The MIME HTML (MHTML) format supported in Internet Explorer and Opera (as well as in Microsoft Word). You need an add-in to work with .mht files in other browsers, including FireFox.

See Also For information about sending pages in different formats via e-mail, see "E-Mailing Pages in Shareable Formats" in Chapter 2.

After you select a format and click Save As, OneNote displays the Save As dialog box. The folder selected in the dialog box is the location where the current notebook is stored. You can navigate to a different folder on your computer or on a network as necessary. You might need to provide your user name and password to save a file to a network location such as a Microsoft SharePoint site.

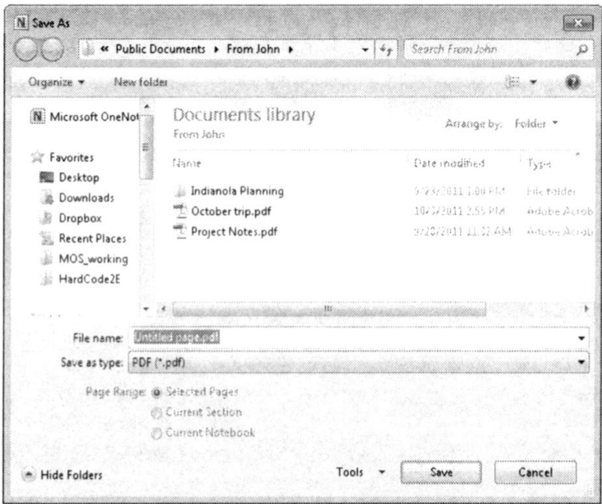

You can change the scope of the content you are saving in the Save As dialog box. Choose an option from the Page Range area to save the current section or current notebook instead of the current page.

Notice the set of option buttons in the Save As dialog box that let you change from saving the current page to saving the current section or the notebook. Choose a different option under Page Range if you now decide to save more content than the current page.

➤ To save the current page in a different format

1. Display the page you want to save.
2. Click **File**, and then click **Save As**.
3. Under **Save Current**, select **Page**.
4. Under **Select Format**, select the format you want to use.
5. Click **Save As**.
6. In the **Save As** dialog box, specify the location where you want to save the page and then click **Save**.

Saving Notebooks in Different File Formats

The formats in which you can save a complete notebook are more limited than for pages or sections. You can save a notebook as a PDF or XPS file or as a OneNote Package, which uses the file name extension (.onepkg).

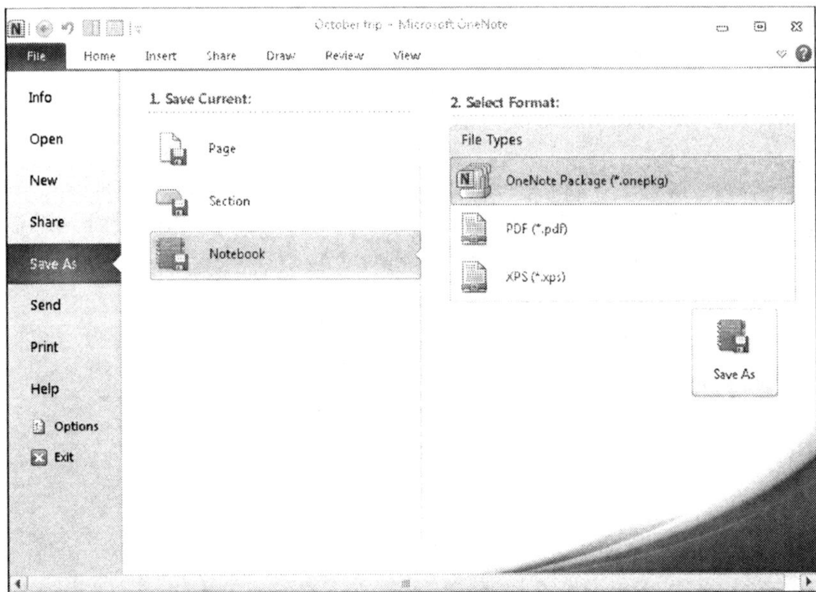

When you double-click PDF, for example, OneNote displays the Save As dialog box. By default, OneNote uses the name of the notebook to name the PDF file. In a PDF file that contains a complete notebook, you'll see a layout similar to a OneNote page, with the page's name and the date and time stamp in the top-left corner. The section names appear in a footer at the bottom of the page. The XPS option provides similarly formatted output.

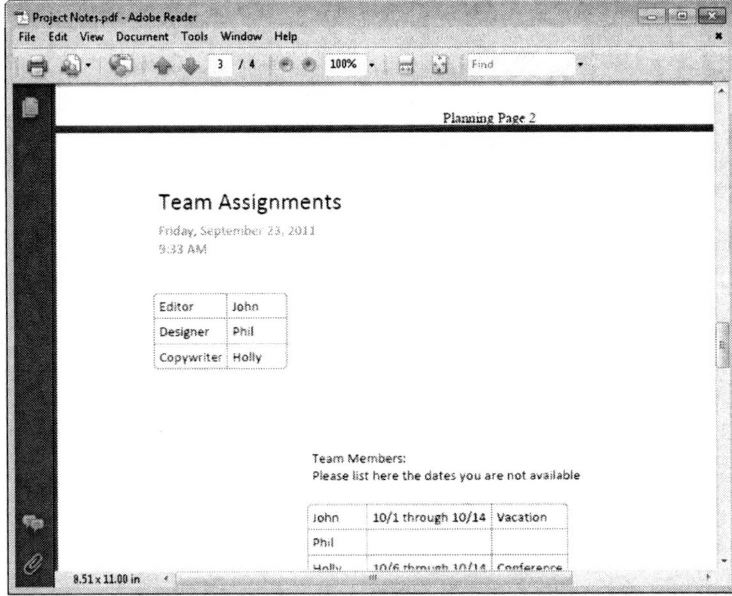

You'll see results like this when you save a notebook in PDF or XPS format.

The option to create a OneNote package file is helpful when you need to move a notebook from one computer to another. Instead of copying the folder that contains the notebook's section files, you can use the OneNote package format to work with a single file.

After you save a package file, you can double-click it to display the Unpack Notebook dialog box. In this dialog box, you can update the notebook's name, select a color for its associated icon, and change the path where the notebook will be created (which initially points to the default location for OneNote notebooks on the local computer).

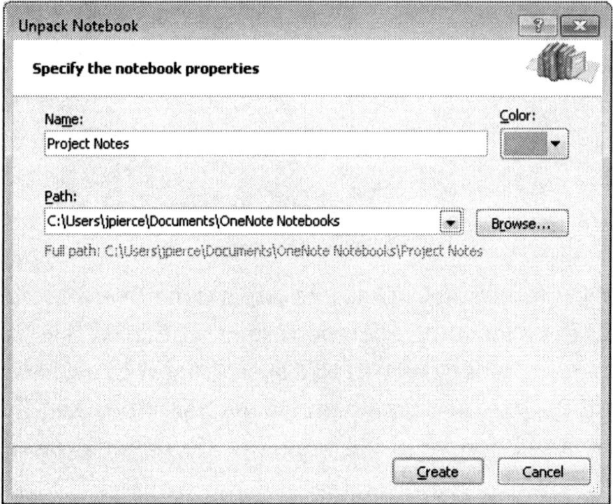

Tip **To import a package file into OneNote, click File and then click Open. Set the file type to OneNote Single File Package, select the saved file, and click Open.**

➤ To save the current notebook in a different format

1. Open the note you want to save.
2. Click **File**, and then click **Save As**.
3. Under **Save Current**, select **Notebook**.
4. Under **Select Format**, select the format you want to use.
5. Click **Save As**.
6. In the **Save As** dialog box, specify the location where you want to save the page and then click **Save**.

Practice Tasks

The practice files for these tasks are located in the practice files folder for Microsoft OneNote 2010. You can save the results of these exercises in the same folder. Change the file name so that you don't overwrite the sample files. When you are done, try performing the following tasks:

- Open the notebook Department Meetings 2011.
- Save the page named August in the Word Document format. Save the December page in the XPS format.
- Save the notebook as a OneNote package file to a different location on your computer, and then unpack the file in that location.

3.5 Use Quick Filing

Many notebooks you create in OneNote contain a mix of elements, such as text notes, images, tables, and drawings. The frequency with which you integrate different types of content in a notebook is evident in how OneNote works directly with other applications, including Microsoft Outlook and Windows Internet Explorer.

See Also In addition to integrating different types of content, you can link notes to applications such as Microsoft Word and Microsoft PowerPoint. For details, see "Linking Notes to Other Applications" in Chapter 4, "Editing and Linking Content in OneNote."

You can add different types of content to OneNote by using commands that are included in other applications (the OneNote button in Outlook, for example) or by using commands in OneNote itself. In the following sections, you'll learn how to send an item such as an appointment from Outlook or a screen clipping from a website to a notebook. You'll also learn how to manage the settings for where OneNote saves these items.

Sending Outlook Items to OneNote

When you are reading e-mail in Outlook, you can use the OneNote command in the Move group on the Outlook ribbon's Home tab to create a note in OneNote that contains details about a message. You can perform the same operation for appointments and meetings, contacts, and tasks.

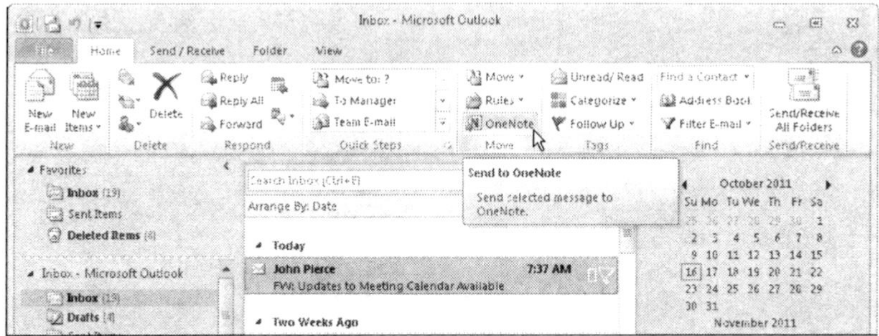

To send the details from an e-mail message to a notebook, click the OneNote button in Outlook. You'll find this button in contact, task, and meeting/appointment items as well.

By default, when you send an item from Outlook to OneNote, OneNote displays the Select Location In OneNote dialog box. The dialog box lists recent locations to which you have sent items and a list of all notebooks (shared and local). For an e-mail message or a task, you can select a section or a page in which to insert the item's details. For a calendar item or a contact, you can select only a section. OneNote adds the item to a new page in the section you choose.

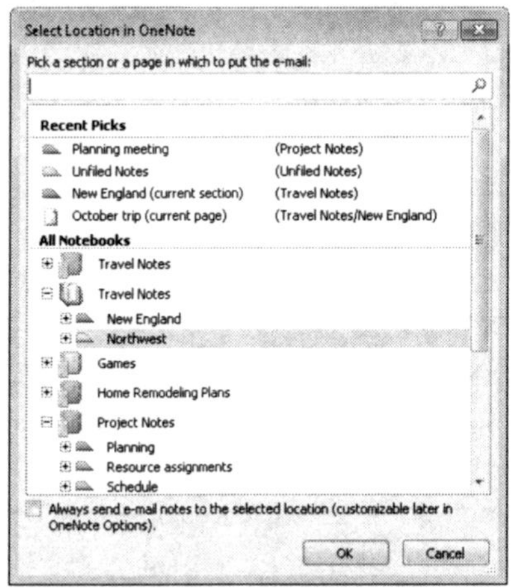

You work with different versions of this dialog box when you send Outlook items to OneNote. Select the section or page where you want to send the item. Select the check box at the bottom of the dialog box to specify a default location.

Notice the option at the bottom of the dialog box. You can select this check box to specify your current choice as the default location for sending items. You can set this option as well in the OneNote Options dialog box. You'll learn more about options for specifying send-to locations later in the chapter.

➤ **To send an Outlook e-mail message to OneNote**

1. Open Outlook and display the e-mail window.
2. In the Inbox or a different folder, select the message or messages you want to send.
3. In the **Move** group on the **Home** tab, click the **OneNote** button.
4. In the **Select Location In OneNote** dialog box, specify the section or page where you want to insert the message details.

➤ **To send an Outlook calendar item, task item, or contact item to OneNote**

1. Open Outlook and display the calendar, task, or contact window.
2. Double-click the item you want to send to OneNote.
3. On the item's ribbon, click the **OneNote** button. (You can find this button on the **Appointment**, **Meeting**, **Task**, or **Contact** tab, as applicable.)
4. In the **Select Location In OneNote** dialog box, specify the section or page where you want to insert the message details.

Sending Web Pages, Screen Clippings, and Printouts to OneNote

Three other types of content you can add to a OneNote notebook are web pages, screen clippings, and printouts. Internet Explorer has a built in Send To OneNote command that appears when you right-click a web page. When you work in another application, you have the option of printing a document or other file to OneNote, and you can add a screen clipping to a OneNote page when you want to preserve or distribute an image from your screen.

Adding Web Content to OneNote

You can also send the content on a web page to OneNote by choosing Send To OneNote from the menu that appears when you right-click the web page in Internet Explorer. (The location of this command might vary depending on which version of Internet Explorer you are using.) You can send the entire page or elements (images or text) that you select on the page.

The default setting for web content is also for OneNote to display the Select Location In OneNote dialog box. Choose where you want the content to appear, and use the check box at the bottom of the dialog box if you want to specify the location as the default location.

➤ To send web content to OneNote from Internet Explorer

1. On the web page, select the content you want to send to OneNote. (Skip this step if you want to send the entire page.)
2. Right-click, and choose **Send To OneNote**.
3. In the **Select Location In OneNote** dialog box, specify the location where you want the content to appear.

Adding a Screen Clipping

The Screen Clipping command appears on the Insert tab. Click this command in OneNote, and you'll see that the OneNote window is minimized and the window behind OneNote appears, with the content in that window dimmed. Drag across the window to select the portion of the screen you want to add to the current page. When you release the mouse button, OneNote becomes the active window, and the screen clipping is added to the current page.

If OneNote isn't running, press the Windows logo key+S to create a screen clipping. When you release the mouse button, OneNote displays the Select Location In OneNote dialog box, in which you can choose a section or page or use the Copy To Clipboard button to preserve the clipping for use in a separate application.

> **Tip** **Screen clippings are tagged with the date and time they are taken. Web pages are also tagged with the page name and the site's URL.**

➤ To add a screen clipping to OneNote

1. Position the window you want to take a clipping from behind OneNote.
2. On the **Insert** tab in OneNote, click **Screen Clipping**.
3. In the window that appears, drag to select the content you want to add, and then release the mouse button.

   The screen clipping is added to the current page.

Printing to OneNote

When you install OneNote, the program sets up a virtual printer named Send To OneNote 2010. You can use this option, for example, to print a PDF file or a PowerPoint slide to a OneNote page.

Open a presentation, an Excel worksheet, or a Word document (for example), display the Print page in Backstage view, and then select Send To OneNote 2010 from the list of printers. Set any other printing options. (In PowerPoint, you might choose to print the current slide or the full presentation and also select a layout—for example, nine slides to a page.) Click Print, and you'll see another version of the Select Location In OneNote dialog box, this one prompting you to indicate where you want to place the printout. You can choose a page or a section in any of the notebooks listed.

➤ To send a printout to OneNote

1. Open the document, worksheet, presentation, or other file that contains the content you want to send to OneNote.
2. On the application's **Print** page or **Print** dialog box, select **Send To OneNote 2010**.
3. Set any printer options (such as page range), and then click **Print**.

Setting Send-To Options

For all of these methods of adding information to a notebook, the default setting is for OneNote to prompt you for the location before the content is added. You can change the settings for one or all of these methods on the Send To OneNote page in the OneNote Options dialog box.

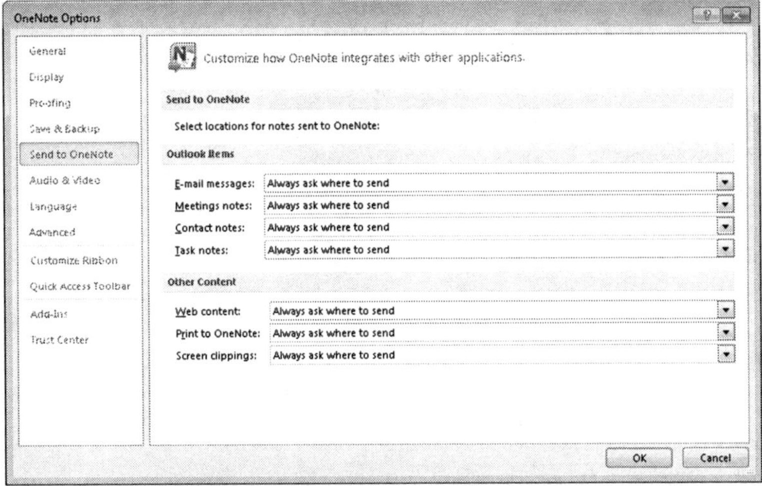

For the items on this page, you can choose from three or four options for how the type of content is sent to OneNote:

- **Always Ask Where To Send** This is the default setting. With this setting selected, OneNote displays the Select Location In OneNote dialog box, where you can designate a specific section or page (depending on the type of content).

- **To Current Page** This option is available for e-mail messages and task notes from Outlook and for web content and printing to OneNote.
- **To New Page In Current Section** This option is available for all types of content.
- **Set Default Location** When you choose this setting, OneNote displays the Select Location In OneNote dialog box. Select the section or page to which you want to send this type of content by default. For example, you might create a notebook named Tasks and send all task items to a section in that notebook.

➤ To configure options for sending content to OneNote

1. Click **File, Options**.
2. In the **OneNote Options** dialog box, display the **Send To OneNote** page.
3. Choose the send-to option for the type of content you are configuring.

Practice Tasks

The practice files for these tasks are located in the practice files folder for Microsoft OneNote 2010. You can save the results of these exercises in the same folder. Change the file name so that you don't overwrite the sample files. When you are done, try performing the following tasks:

- If you have access to Microsoft Outlook on your computer, practice sending different items to a notebook in OneNote.
- Use the Screen Clipping command to add a screen shot to a notebook.
- Open the Word document OneNote_Printout.docx, and then use the Send To OneNote 2010 printer to add a printout to a notebook.

3.6 Use and Manage Tags

Many of the notes you add to a notebook have common attributes. By using the tags feature in OneNote, you can identify and categorize similar types of notes. You can, for example, apply a tag to identify each note you want to add to your to-do list, discuss with your manager, or forward in e-mail to one of your coworkers or a friend. The menu of built-in tags that OneNote provides gives you a wide range of choices, and you can add your own tags as well as modify the built-in ones.

Assigning a tag to a note is the first step you take in using tags as an organizational tool. With a set of tagged notes, you can then use commands in OneNote to create a summary of tagged notes and search for notes by tags.

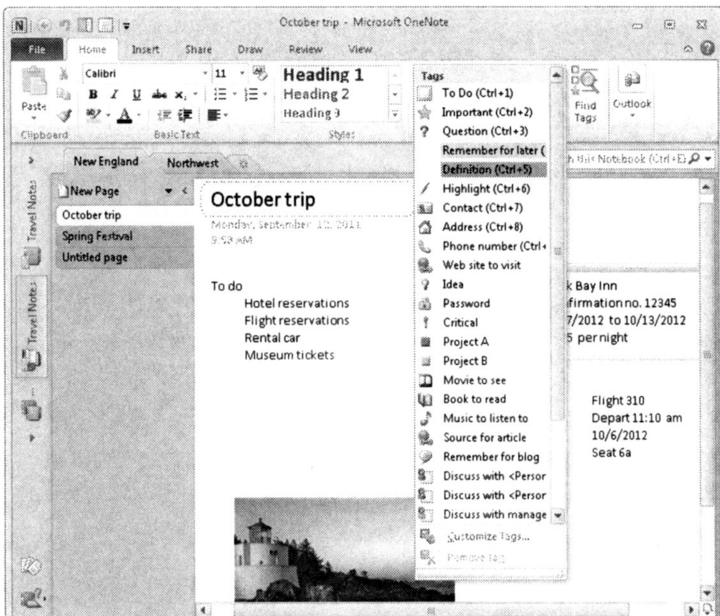

The built-in tags in OneNote serve as starting points for the types of tags you can create and apply to categorize your notes. Click Customize Tags when you want to define a tag of your own.

Tags are represented by symbols—a question mark, a check box for the To Do tag, a light bulb for an idea you record as part of a brainstorming session, for example—or, in two cases, by highlighting (the Remember For Later and Definition tags). When you create tags of your own, you can choose a symbol, a font color, and whether to apply colored highlighting.

In the following sections, you'll learn the ins and outs of using tags to help organize your work in OneNote.

Applying Tags to Paragraphs

You can apply one or more tags (as many as nine) to each paragraph in a note container. (If you select a note container and apply a tag to it, the tag is applied to each paragraph in the container.) You can also apply a tag as the first step in creating a note. For example, click on a page, choose an applicable tag from the menu, and then type or write the note.

Keyboard Shortcuts for Tags

When you open the Tags menu, you'll see that the first nine tags are associated with a keyboard shortcut (Ctrl+1 through Ctrl+9). You can apply the related tags by pressing the keyboard combination assigned to it. For example, press Ctrl+3 to assign the Question tag to a paragraph. If you want to change which tag is assigned to a keyboard shortcut, click Customize Tags at the bottom of the Tags menu, and then use the Move Tag Up and Move Tag Down buttons to change the order in which tags are listed. The first nine tags in that list are assigned to the Ctrl key combinations.

When you want to remove a tag from a paragraph, select the paragraph, open the Tags menu, and then click Remove Tag. You also have three alternatives: select the tagged paragraph and press Ctrl+0; right-click the tag and then choose Remove Tag from the shortcut menu; or right-click the tagged paragraph, click Tag, and then click Remove Tag.

➤ To apply a tag

1. Click in the paragraph you want to assign a tag to.
2. On the **Home** tab, open the **Tags** menu and then select the tag you want to apply.

➤ To remove a tag

→ Right-click the tag icon, and choose **Remove Tag**.

Creating Custom Tags

At the bottom of the Tags menu, click Customize Tags to begin the steps you follow to define a tag of your own. In the Customize Tags dialog box, click New Tag.

In the New Tag dialog box, enter a display name for the tag. Then, using the Symbol, Font Color, and Highlight Color controls, define the visual properties for the tag. Under Symbol, choose None or one of the many choices that OneNote provides. You can choose one of 40 font colors and from 15 options for a highlight. The selections you make are shown in the Preview area of the New Tag dialog box.

➤ To create a custom tag

1. On the **Home** tab, open the **Tags** menu and then click **Customize Tags**.
2. In the **Customize Tags** dialog box, click **New Tag**.
3. In the **New Tag** dialog box, type a name for the tag.
4. Select the symbol, font color, and highlight you want to use to define the tag. (You don't need to use each of these formatting options.)

Modifying Tags

To modify a tag—either a built-in tag or one you have defined—click Customize Tags in the Tags menu and then click Modify Tag in the Customize Tags dialog box. The Modify Tag dialog box appears next. This dialog box contains the same set of controls as the New Tag dialog box. You can update the display name for the tag you are modifying and also make changes to the symbol that represents the tag, font color, and highlight color.

Important Note the statement just above the OK and Cancel buttons in the Modify Tag dialog box. If you change the appearance of the built-in To Do tag, for example, the tag's appearance doesn't change for notes to which you've already applied the tag. You'll see the modified tag when you apply the tag from this point forward.

➤ **To modify a tag**

1. On the **Home** tab, open the **Tags** menu and then click **Customize Tags**.
2. In the **Customize Tags** dialog box, select the tag you want to modify and then click **Modify Tag**.
3. In the **Modify Tag** dialog box, make changes to the display name, symbol, font color, and highlight color that define the tag.

Finding Tags

When you click Find Tags in the Home tab's Tags group, OneNote displays the Tags Summary pane and lists each tagged note in open notebooks under a heading for the tag—all To Do notes are grouped together, for example, as are all the notes tagged Important.

OneNote groups tags in the Tags Summary pane. Use the Group Tabs By list to change how the tags are arranged. Use the Search list to set the search scope (for pages, sections, notebooks, or time intervals).

You can use the Tags Summary pane to locate notes in a particular category. The tag groups can be collapsed and expanded to make your view of the notes in a group more concise. To display the page that contains the tagged note, click its entry in the tag groupings.

You can also change the view and the results shown in the Tags Summary pane. Use the Group By list to change from Tag Name (the default view) to Section, Title, Date, or Note Text.

In the Search list below the tag groupings, you can select the scope and the time period you want to use to locate notes. For the search scope, you can choose from This Page Group, This Section, This Section Group, This Notebook, and All Notebooks. For time periods, you can choose from Today's Notes, Yesterday's Notes, This Week's Notes, Last Week's Notes, and Older Notes. Click Refresh Results after changing the setting in the Search list to update the results in the Tags Summary pane.

➤ **To find tags**

1. On the **Home** tab, in the **Tags** group, click **Find Tags**.
2. In the **Tags Summary** pane, expand and collapse the tag groups if necessary to locate the type of tag you are looking for.
3. Use the **Group Tags By** list to change how tags are sorted.
4. Use the **Search** list to change the scope for the tag summary.
5. Click **Refresh Results** to update the **Tags Summary** pane.

Creating a Tag Summary Page

A tags summary page displays all tagged notes in a section on their own page. Click Create Summary Page in the Tags Summary pane to collect tagged notes on this page. OneNote adds a page to the end of the current section (in a single note container) where you can check off to-do items, for example, or review notes with other types of tags.

The entries on the tag summary page are copies that are linked to the original notes. When you point to a tagged note on the summary page, a OneNote icon appears, and you can click the icon to display the original note. Although the summary notes are linked to the originals, they are not synchronized copies. This means that if you remove a tag on the summary page or select the check box for a tagged note, the action you take does not change the original note. In addition, notes you add to a section are not automatically added to the summary page.

> **Tip** Clicking Create Summary Page a second time creates a second summary page. It does not update a summary page already in the notebook.

➤ To create a tag summary page

1. On the **Home** tab, click **Find Tags** in the **Tags** group.
2. In the **Tags Summary** pane, click **Create Summary Page**.

Configuring Tag Options

A few options for configuring tags appear on the Advanced page in the OneNote Options dialog box. The options relate to how OneNote displays original tags when you create a tag summary page.

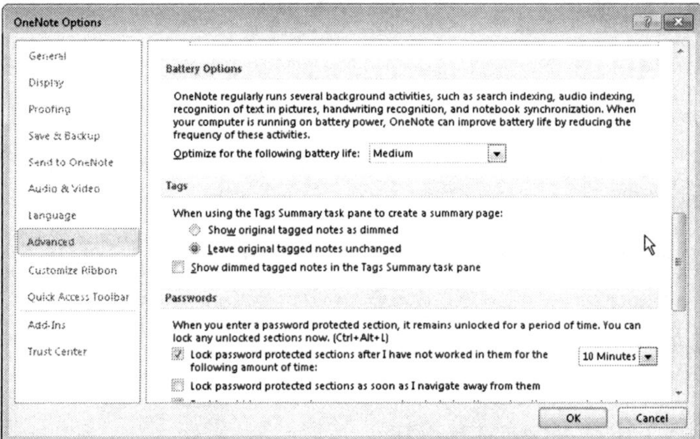

With the default settings (Leave Original Tagged Notes Unchanged), OneNote shows tagged notes as you see them when you first apply the tags—in other words, tagged notes are displayed the same on the tags summary page and on the pages that contain the original notes. If you select the option Show Original Tagged Notes As Dimmed, the tagged notes appear as they normally do on the tag summary page but are dimmed on the original pages.

Selecting the check box for the last option for configuring tags—Show Dimmed Tagged Notes In The Tags Summary Task Pane—causes OneNote to include dimmed tags from the original page and the normal tag from the tag summary page. By selecting this option, you essentially create duplicate entries for tags.

➤ To configure options for tagged notes

1. Click **File**, **Options**.
2. In the **OneNote Options** dialog box, click the **Advanced** page.
3. Scroll to the **Tags** area, and then select the options you want to use for showing original and dimmed tags.

Practice Tasks

The practice files for these tasks are located in the practice files folder for Microsoft OneNote 2010. You can save the results of these exercises in the same folder. Change the file name so that you don't overwrite the sample files. When you are done, try performing the following tasks:

- Open the notebook Budget Planning.
- Apply several of the built-in tags to notes in the Division Goals section.
- Create a custom tag named Sales Opportunity.
- Modify the built-in Project A tag. Change the display name to Expense, and change its font properties.
- Use the Tag Summary pane to search for notes referring to the Marketing department.
- Create a tag summary page. Use the links on the summary page to navigate to the original notes.

Objective Review

Before finishing this chapter, be sure you have mastered the following skills:

- Use OneNote notebook organizational tools
- Search OneNote
- Use history and backups in OneNote
- Use the Save As command
- Use quick filing
- Use and manage tags

4 Editing and Linking Content in OneNote

The skills tested in this section of the Microsoft Office Specialist exam for Microsoft OneNote 2010 are related to editing and linking content. Specifically, the following objectives are associated with this set of skills:

4.1 Use links and linked notes
4.2 Insert files
4.3 Edit text in OneNote
4.4 Insert and modify visual elements

In this chapter, you'll learn about hands-on steps you take to edit and add various types of content to a notebook. In the chapter's first section, you'll learn about creating links between notes, pages, sections, and notebooks, and about creating linked notes, including notes you can link to documents in Microsoft Word and Microsoft PowerPoint and to web pages in Internet Explorer. The chapter's later sections describe procedures for inserting files, how you edit and format text in notes, and how to work with visual elements such as pictures, special symbols, and drawings.

4.1 Use Links and Linked Notes

In the following sections, you'll learn how to create different types of links in OneNote. Linking pages to other pages, linking notes to pages or sections or notebooks, as well as linking notes to documents created in other applications are various ways in which you can deepen the associations between the content you include in a OneNote notebook.

Linking Pages to Other OneNote Pages

Linking one page to another provides the means by which you can quickly navigate through a notebook, create relationships between pages, and cut down on any information that might seem redundant.

The Copy Link To Page command appears when you right-click a page in the page tabs bar. (You'll see a similar command—Copy Link To Section—when you right-click a section title in the Navigation bar.) Display the page to which you want to add the link, right-click the page, and then click Paste on the Home tab (or simply press Ctrl+V). If you click the Paste button, it's best to choose the Keep Source Formatting or Merge Formatting option. With one of these options, OneNote displays the link by using the page title as the display text. If you choose Keep Text Only, you'll still get a working link, but the link's display text is the lengthy ID OneNote uses to refer to the page.

> **Tip** By default, links to pages are shown in a blue font with a solid underline. Links to subpages are displayed in a blue font with dashed underlining. You can apply other formatting to a link by selecting it and then applying a style or by using the basic text formatting tools on the Home tab.

To modify a link, right-click the link and choose Edit Link. This opens the Link dialog box. (See "Linking to Files" later in this chapter for more information.) Here you can choose a different page or section for the link. You can also use this dialog box to modify the display text. Use the Copy Link, Select Link, and Remove Link commands on this shortcut menu to manage the link as necessary.

➤ To link a page to another page

1. In the page tabs bar, right-click the page and then choose **Copy Link To Page**.
2. Open the page on which you want to insert the link, and then press Ctrl+V to paste the link.

Linking Notes to Pages, Sections, Notebooks, and Wikilinks

In addition to using the Copy Link To Page command to link one page to another, you can use variations of this command to link notes to pages, sections, and notebooks. You can also create a link by typing a pair of square brackets around a page name or a section name (something like **[[PlanningUpdate]]**) to create a wikilink. In the following sections, you'll learn how to create these types of links.

Using the Copy Link To Command

To link a note to a page, section, section group, or notebook, right-click the item in the page tabs bar or the Navigation bar and then choose the Copy Link To command. The command's full name reflects the item you are linking to—Copy Link To Page, Copy Link To Section, Copy Link To Section Group, and Copy Link To Notebook.

> **Tip** Right-click a paragraph in a note container and choose Copy Link To Paragraph to create a link to a specific note.

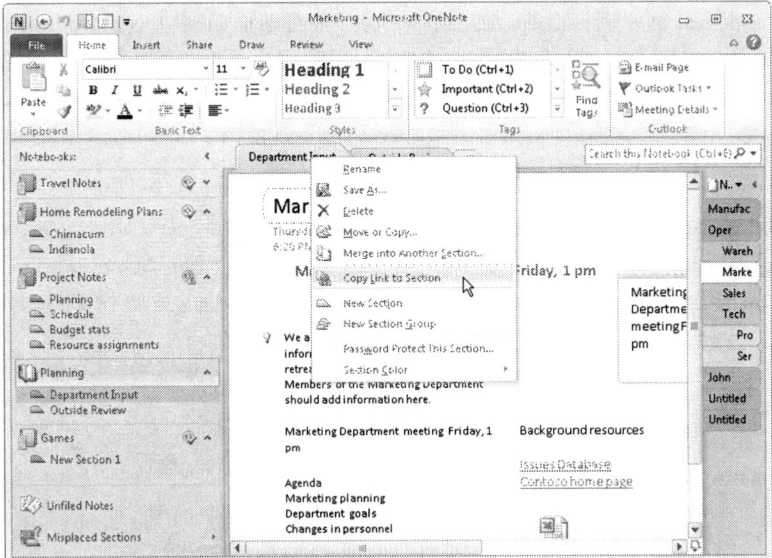

Use the Copy Link To command to link a note to a page, section, section group, or notebook.

After copying the link to the destination, display the note (which could be a note you added previously or a new note) in which you want to include the link and press Ctrl+V to paste the link.

Right-click a link you've added to open a shortcut menu from which you can choose a command to copy the link, select the link (to format it, for example), or remove the link. The Edit Link command on this menu opens the Link dialog box. You can use this dialog box to change the display text for the link or to select another location.

> **See Also** For more information about working in the Link dialog box, see "Linking to Files" later in this chapter.

➤ To link a note to a page, section, section group, or notebook

1. In the Navigation bar or page tab bars, right-click the item you want to link the note to.
2. From the shortcut menu, choose the **Copy Link To** command.
3. Display the note in which you want to insert the link, and then press Ctrl+V to paste the link.

Creating a Wikilink

By enclosing text in a pair of square brackets, such as [[*text*]], you can link a note to a page or a section in a notebook or to another notebook. Just enter the name of the notebook, page, or section as the text between the brackets. (This technique is also used to create links in some wiki pages on websites.) The page or section can be in the same notebook or in a different one. If the page or section is in a notebook that is closed, OneNote opens the notebook when you click the link.

You can also use the wikilink syntax to create a page and a link to that page at the same time. To do this, enter the text you want to use as a page's title (which can't duplicate an existing page) between the brackets. OneNote creates the page in the current section.

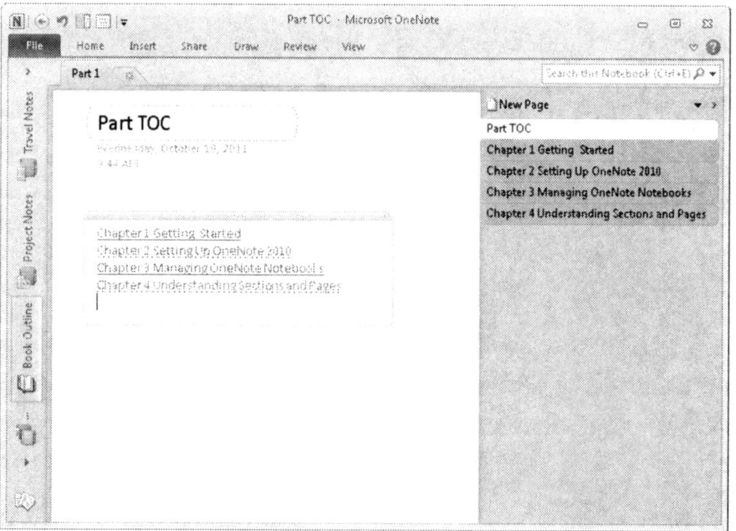

You can create a new page and link to it by enclosing the page title in double square brackets.

➤ To create a wikilink to a notebook, page, or section

→ Type two left square brackets, type the page or section title, and then type two right square brackets—for example, [[*SectionTitle*]].

➤ To create a page and a link to the new page

→ Type two left square brackets, type the text you want to use for the page title, and then type two right square brackets.

Working with Side Notes and Docked Windows

In Chapter 3, "Organizing and Finding Notes," in the section "Using Side Notes," you learned about creating a side note by using the OneNote icon that appears by default in the Windows taskbar. You can also create a side note when you are working in OneNote by using the New Side Note command on the View tab.

The New Docked Window command, also on the View tab, docks a second OneNote window (by default, at the right side of the screen) and enables linked notes. Linked notes are a tool by which you can link notes to specific locations in OneNote, as well as to documents in Microsoft Word and Microsoft PowerPoint and to web pages you view in Internet Explorer.

See Also For detailed information about creating linked notes in Word, PowerPoint, and Internet Explorer, see "Linking Notes to Other Applications" later in this chapter.

The advantage of using linked notes is that the link between a note and the reference or location you want to link the note to is created automatically when you enter a note in the docked OneNote window (assuming that you haven't turned off linked notes). With linked notes, you can do research in one application (reviewing the content in another OneNote notebook, for example), type a note in the docked window, and then later use the link to open the notebook you were using for research.

Adding a Side Note from OneNote

To insert a side note, click New Side Note in the View tab's Window group. Use the side note window that OneNote displays to record your note. Keep the window open to add to the side note. When you close the window, OneNote adds the side note to the Unfiled Notes section. OneNote creates a page under Unfiled Notes for each side note you record.

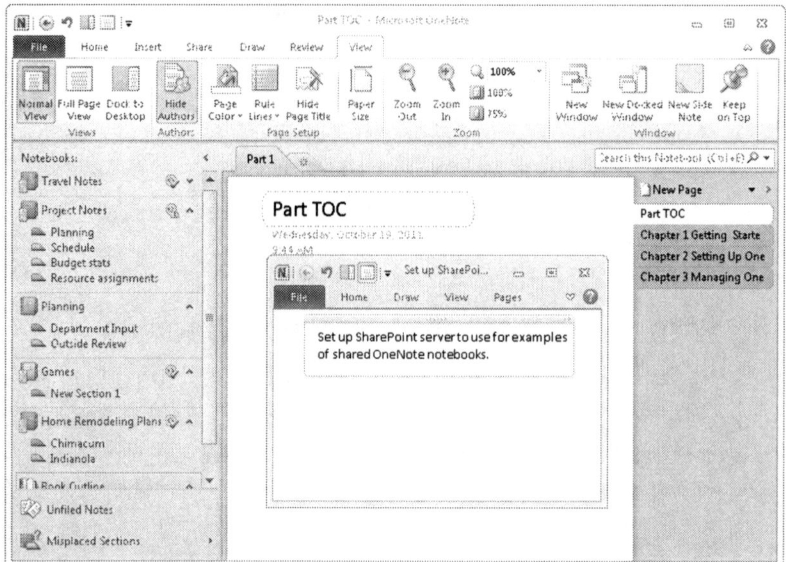

Side notes are initially saved under Unfiled Notes. OneNote stores each side note on a separate page.

➤ To insert a side note from OneNote

1. On the **View** tab, click **New Side Note**.
2. In the side note window, type the note.
3. Close the side note window.
4. Move the note from the **Unfiled Notes** section to the notebook where you want to save the note.

Working with Linked Notes in a Docked OneNote Window

Click New Docked Window to dock a second OneNote window (which displays the current page) along the right side of the screen. Choosing this command also enables linked notes, which is indicated by the link icon at the top-left corner of the docked window. Notice also that the OneNote ribbon changes its configuration in the docked window. (This change also occurs when you choose Dock To Desktop in the Views group.) The Insert, Share, and Review tabs are no longer included; the Home, Draw, and View tabs include a subset of their regular commands; and the ribbon now includes the Pages tab, which you can use to navigate from page to page in the docked window, add new pages, delete a page, or move the current page to a new location.

Working with Linked Notes

The page on which you record linked notes must be in a section that is saved in the OneNote 2010 section format. You cannot create linked notes on a page that's stored in the OneNote 2007 section format.

Click the down arrow below the linked note icon (in the top-left corner of the docked OneNote window) to display a menu that lets you open a linked file, delete one or more links on the linked note page, stop taking linked notes (and resume taking linked notes again), and set linked note options.

Linked note options appear on the Advanced page of the OneNote Options dialog box. Clear the check box for Allow Creation Of New Linked Notes if you want to turn off the linked notes feature. Clear the check box for the document snippet option if you don't want OneNote to include identifying text with the linked note. Click Remove Links From Linked Notes to remove links from the current notebook. (OneNote prompts you to confirm this operation before the links are removed.)

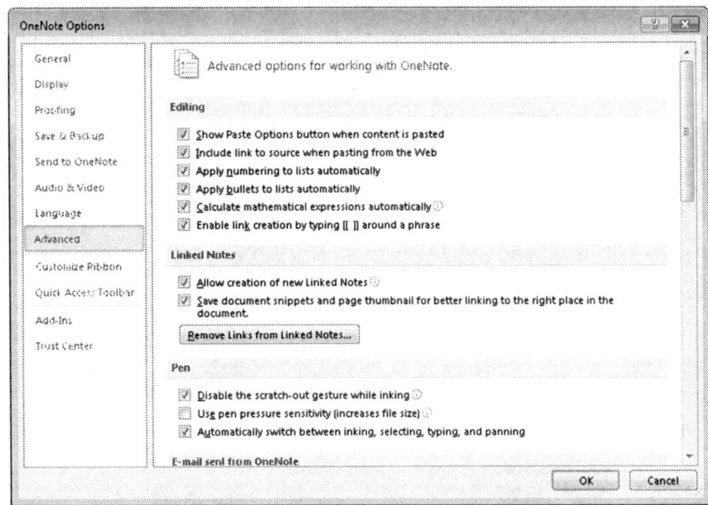

Set options for using linked notes on the Advanced page of the OneNote Options dialog box.

By right-clicking the OneNote icon (or the program icon that appears with linked notes you create in Word, PowerPoint, or Internet Explorer), you open a menu that lets you open the linked file, copy the link, change the destination of the link, remove the link, and set linked note options.

To create a linked note that refers to another page in a OneNote notebook, click New Docked Window to enable linked notes. If you use keyboard shortcuts, press Ctrl+Alt+D to dock the window. In the docked window, display the page to which you want to add linked notes. In the main OneNote window, open the page you want the linked notes to refer to.

When you start typing a note in the docked window, you'll see the OneNote program icon displayed to the left of the note container. Point to this icon to see which page the linked note refers to. Click this icon to activate the link and jump to the page.

➤ To create a linked note in OneNote

1. On the **View** tab, in the **Window** group, click **New Docked Window**.
2. In the docked window, open the page to which you want to add linked notes.
3. In the main OneNote window, display the page you want the linked notes to refer to.
4. Type the note in the docked window.
5. Click the OneNote icon beside the linked note to open the page the note is linked to.

Linking Notes to Other Applications

Linked notes are also supported in Microsoft Word, Microsoft PowerPoint, and Internet Explorer. In each of these applications, the steps you follow to create linked notes are generally the same. In the following sections, you'll learn more about the details for linking notes to documents, presentations, and web pages.

Tip You can create linked notes only to Word documents and PowerPoint presentations that have been saved.

Linking Notes in Word Documents

To start using linked notes in Word 2010, click Linked Notes in the OneNote group on the Review tab in Word. The first time you start taking linked notes in a document, OneNote displays the Select Location In OneNote dialog box. Use this dialog box to specify the OneNote page on which you want the linked notes to appear. You can also choose a section, in which case OneNote creates a new page to store the linked notes.

> **Tip** After you create linked notes in a document, the page associated with the linked notes is opened automatically in OneNote.

When you start typing a note in the docked OneNote window, OneNote adds the Word icon to the left of the note to indicate that the note is linked to the document. When you point to the icon, OneNote displays a ScreenTip that includes a short passage of the text near the insertion point. To associate a specific passage of text with a linked note, select the text in Word and then type the note in OneNote.

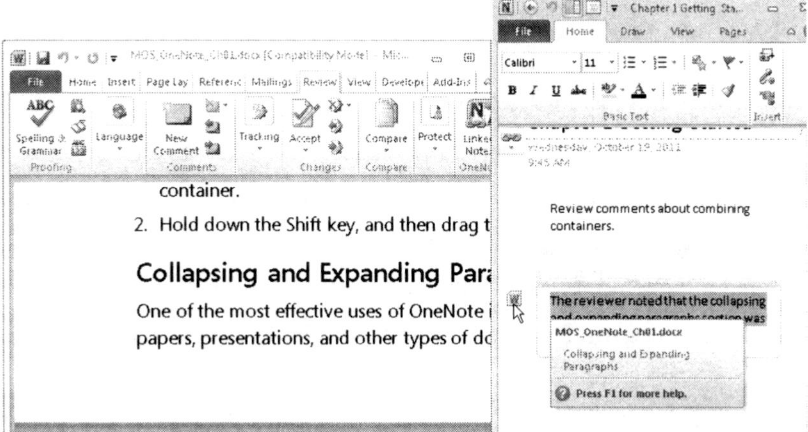

Word, PowerPoint, and Internet Explorer also support linked notes. Click the program icon (the Word icon is shown here) to display the area of the document the note is linked to.

➤ To link notes to a Word document

1. Open the Word document you want to link notes to.

   You can link notes only to a document that has been saved. If you create a new document, save it before you go to step 2.

2. On the **Review** tab in Word, click **Linked Notes**.
3. If necessary, use the **Select Location In OneNote** dialog box to specify the page on which to store linked notes.
4. Scroll to the location in the document you want the linked note to refer to.
5. In the docked OneNote window, type the note.

Linking Notes in PowerPoint Presentations

You follow essentially the same steps to create notes linked to a PowerPoint presentation. In PowerPoint, open the presentation you want to work with, and then click Linked Notes in the OneNote group on the Review tab. You need to select a location (using the Select Location In OneNote dialog box) if this is the first time you've created linked notes for this presentation. If you have created linked notes previously, OneNote opens the associated page.

Display the slide you want to link a note to, and then type a note in the docked OneNote window. OneNote adds the PowerPoint icon to the left side of the note container to indicate that the note is linked.

➤ To link notes to a PowerPoint presentation

1. Open the PowerPoint presentation you want to link notes to.

   You can link notes only to a presentation that has been saved. If you create a new presentation, save it before you go to step 2.
2. On the **Review** tab in PowerPoint, click **Linked Notes**.
3. If necessary, use the **Select Location In OneNote** dialog box to specify the page on which to store linked notes.
4. Scroll to the location in the presentation you want the linked note to refer to.
5. In the docked OneNote window, type the note.

Linking Notes in Internet Explorer

In Internet Explorer 9, you can find the OneNote Linked Notes icon on the command bar. (Right-click to the right of the address box and then choose Command Bar to display the icon.) You can also right-click on a page and then choose OneNote Linked Notes. Go to the page you want to link to a note, and then type the note in the docked OneNote window. Point to the Internet Explorer icon that OneNote adds to indicate that the note is linked, and the ScreenTip shows the URL for the web page and the web page's title.

➤ To link notes to a web page displayed in Internet Explorer

1. Right-click the web page, and choose **OneNote Linked Notes**.
2. If necessary, use the **Select Location In OneNote** dialog box to specify the page on which to store linked notes.
3. In the docked OneNote window, type the note.

Practice Tasks

The practice files for these tasks are located in the practice files folder for Microsoft OneNote 2010. You can save the results of these exercises in the same folder. Change the file name so that you don't overwrite the sample files. When you are done, try performing the following tasks:

- Open the notebook Budget Planning.
- Link the Marketing page to the Manufacturing page.
- Copy the link to the Revenue section, and insert the link in a new note.
- Create a section named FY13, and then use the wikilink syntax to create pages named Q1, Q2, Q3, and Q4.
- Open the Word document Forecast.docx. Create several linked notes that refer to this document. (You can make up text for the content of the notes.)

4.2 Insert Files

You can extend the information that's collected in and accessible through a OneNote notebook by linking to an external file or a website or by embedding a file in a notebook. You can also add a printout of a file to OneNote (by using the built-in Send To OneNote 2010 printer driver) or insert an image from a scanner or a digital camera that's connected to your computer. If you link to or embed a file, you can open the file to make updates—the content you add to the notebook is live. On the other hand, the printouts and scanned images you insert are static representations of the files you used. The commands for inserting files and printouts are located on the OneNote ribbon's Insert tab, in the Links and Files groups.

Linking to Files

The Link command opens a dialog box in which you can specify a website, file, or location in OneNote that you want to link to from the current page. The dialog box also provides a text box in which you can enter display text to identify the link. For example, you could use the display text Home Page to identify a link rather than a URL such as http://www.myhomepage.net.

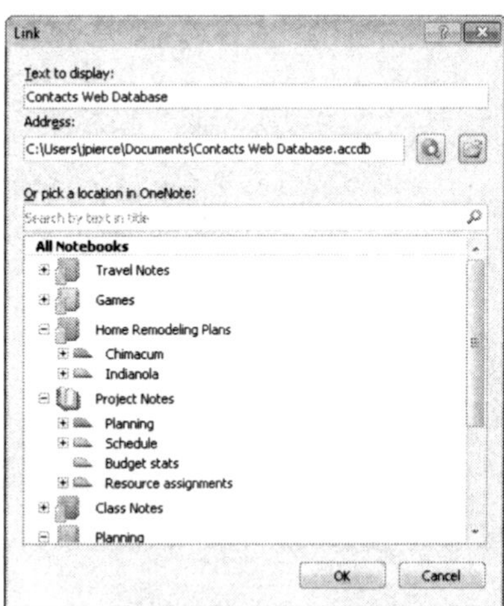

The Link dialog box provides options for linking to web pages, files, and other locations in OneNote.

To link to a website, type the site's URL in the Address box or click the Browse The Web button to open your default web browser and then navigate to the site. Copy the URL in the browser's address box, close the browser (or switch to OneNote), and then paste the URL into the Address box in the Link dialog box. Add the display text you want to provide for the link (for websites, OneNote does not provide any display text by default), and click OK to add the link to the current page.

To link to a file on your local computer or on a network, type the path to the file or click the Browse For File button to open the Link To File dialog box. Open the location where the file is stored, select the file, and then click OK. For files, OneNote inserts the file's name (without the file name extension) in the Text To Display box. Modify the display text if necessary.

The Link dialog box also lets you insert a link to another OneNote notebook, to a section, or to a page. In the Link dialog box, select the notebook, section, or page from the list provided under All Notebooks. (The list shows all open notebooks, not all notebooks stored on your computer.) Use the plus and minus signs to expand and collapse the items that are displayed. You can also search for a location in OneNote by typing the title of a notebook, section, or page in the search box. OneNote filters the list of locations on the basis of the text you type. By default, OneNote uses the display name of the notebook or the title of the section or page for the link's display text. Change or add to the text if necessary.

Below the All Notebooks list is the Create New Page area. Select New Page In Current Section (and enter display text) if you want to link to a new page from the current page. OneNote creates an untitled page in the current section.

➤ To insert a link to a website

1. On the **Insert** tab, click **Link**.
2. In the **Link** dialog box, type the URL for the site in the **Address** box or click the **Browse The Web** button to open your default web browser so that you can go to the site, copy the URL, and paste it into the **Address** box.
3. In the **Text To Display** box, type the text you want to use to identify the link.

➤ To insert a link to a file

1. On the **Insert** tab, click **Link**.
2. In the **Link** dialog box, type the path to the file in the **Address** box or click the **Browse For File** button to open the **Link To File** dialog box.
3. In the **Link To File** dialog box, open the location where the file is stored, select the file, and then click **OK.**
4. In the **Text To Display** box, make any changes you want to the text that OneNote provides to identify the link.

➤ To insert a link to a location in OneNote

1. On the **Insert** tab, click **Link**.
2. In the **Link** dialog box, select the notebook, section, or page under **All Notebooks**, or use the search box provided to find the location you want.
3. In the **Text To Display** box, make any changes you want to the text that OneNote provides to identify the link.

➤ To insert a link to a new page in the current section

1. On the **Insert** tab, click **Link**.
2. In the **Link** dialog box, under **Create New Page**, select **New Page In Current Section**.
3. In the **Text To Display** box, make any changes you want to the text that OneNote provides to identify the link.

Embedding Files

In the Insert tab's Files group, the Attach File command lets you attach (or embed) a file in a notebook. When you click Attach File, OneNote displays the Choose A File Or A Set Of Files To Insert dialog box. Select a single file, or press and hold Ctrl or Shift to select a group of files. (Press Ctrl to select a set of noncontiguous files; press Shift to select more than one file listed contiguously.) OneNote displays embedded files as icons on the current page, and the icon is labeled with the file's name.

> **Tip** When you double-click an icon to open the file, OneNote displays a warning that opening an attachment could harm your computer. Select the option Don't Show This Again before you click OK in the warning to forego this step in the future.

Embedded Files and OneNote Section File Size

OneNote stores a copy of a file you embed in a notebook in the section's .one file. This means that the size of the .one file increases by the size of the embedded file. If you delete an embedded file, the size of the .one file won't decrease immediately, although you might expect it to. OneNote will optimize the file later to account for the deleted file, but you can perform this operation yourself in the OneNote Options dialog box. Click File, Options to open the dialog box. Display the Save & Backup page, and then click Optimize All Files Now.

➤ To embed a file in a notebook

1. On the **Insert** tab, click **Attach File**.
2. In the **Choose A File Or A Set Of Files To Insert** dialog box, select the file or files you want to embed and then click **Insert**.

Printing Files to OneNote

When OneNote is installed, a virtual printer is set up along with the program. You can see this "printer," named Send To OneNote 2010, by opening the Devices And Printers folder from the Start menu in Windows 7. You can use the Send To OneNote 2010 virtual printer to add a printout to a OneNote notebook when you are working in OneNote or when you are working in another application. Add a printout if you want to insert the content of a file and preserve its formatting—so that it appears as though you had printed it on paper.

If you are working in OneNote, OneNote opens the document's original application and then "prints" and inserts the document automatically. You don't need to make any additional settings in the Print dialog box. In addition to displaying the document's content, OneNote embeds a copy of the file and provides a link you can use to open the document.

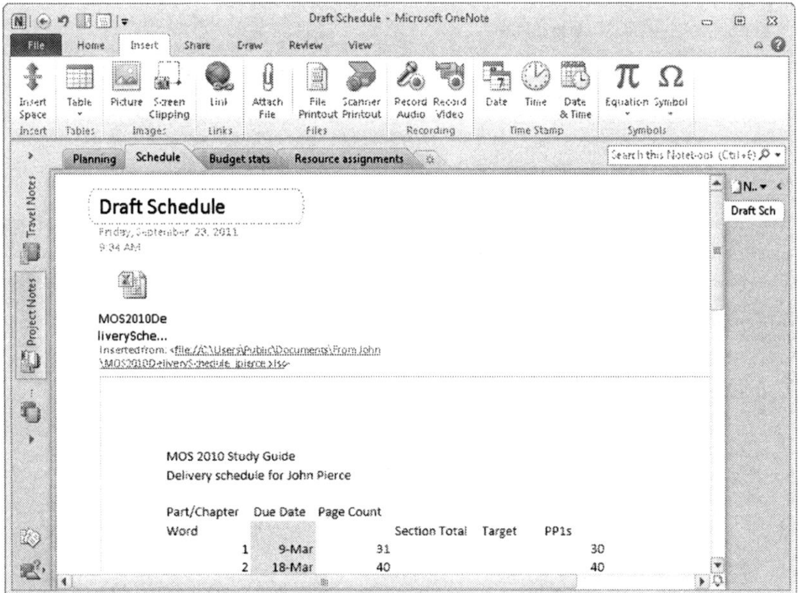

When you insert a printout of a file from OneNote, OneNote attaches the file and includes a link in addition to creating the printout.

You can use the icon or the link to open the original document and edit it. (Be sure, of course, to save the document in the original application if you want to preserve any changes you make.) Modifications you make to the document are not reflected in the printout, which is a static representation of the file in the state it was when you inserted it.

When you are working in another application—another Office application or an application such as Adobe Acrobat or your web browser, for example—you can choose the Send To OneNote 2010 printer driver in the Print dialog box (or on the Print page in Backstage view) to insert a printout in a notebook. Choose the Print command in the application, choose Send To OneNote 2010 from the list of printers, and then make any other print settings you want to apply—a specific page range, for example. When you print the document, OneNote displays the Select Location In OneNote dialog box. Use this dialog box to specify the section or page where you want to add the printout. In this case, only a representation of the file is included on the page you select. OneNote does not also embed the file or provide a link.

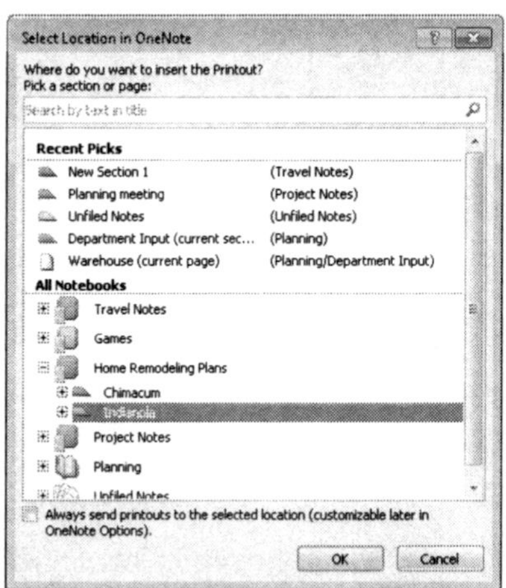

When you insert a printout from another application's Print menu, you need to specify a location for the printout in OneNote.

➤ **To insert a printout in a notebook from OneNote**

1. On the **Insert** tab, click **File Printout**.
2. In the **Choose Document To Insert** dialog box, select the file and then click **Insert**.

➤ **To send a file printout to OneNote from another application**

1. In the application, open the **Print** dialog box (or the **Print** page in Backstage view if you are working with another Office 2010 application).
2. From the list of printers, select **Send To OneNote 2010**, and then click **Print**.
3. In the **Select Location In OneNote** dialog box, specify the page where you want the printout to appear and then click **OK**.

Inserting a Printout from a Scanner or a Camera

If you have a scanner or a digital camera attached to your computer, you can scan an image directly to OneNote. On the Insert tab, click Scanner Printout, which opens the Insert Picture From Scanner Or Camera dialog box.

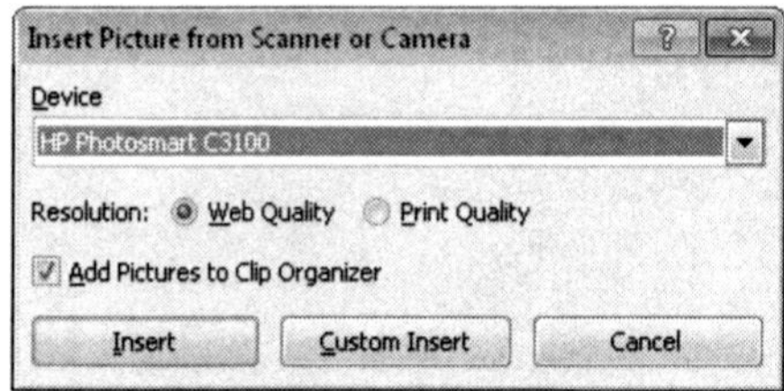

Use this dialog box to specify settings for a printout you insert from a scanner. Click Custom Insert to see more options.

Choose the device and the resolution you want to use. Choose Print Quality resolution if you want an image with better resolution. Keep the Add Pictures To Clip Organizer option selected if you want to make the image you scan part of the collection of clip art available on your computer.

> **Tip** You can open the Clip Organizer by clicking Start, All Programs, Microsoft Office, Microsoft Office 2010 Tools, Microsoft Clip Organizer. Images you scan with the Add Pictures To Clip Organizer option selected should be available in the My Collections area of the Collection List, stored under the name of the device.

Click Insert to scan the image with default settings. Click Custom Insert to open a dialog box in which you can choose options to create a color or black-and-white image and set other options for the quality of the scanned image. The options in this dialog box depend on the device you are using.

➤ To insert an image from a scanner or a camera

1. On the **Insert** tab, click **Scanner Printout**.
2. In the **Insert Image From Scanner Or Camera** dialog box, select the device and resolution you want to use.
3. Click **Insert**, or click **Custom Insert** to display a dialog box in which you can specify additional options before scanning the image.

Practice Tasks

The practice files for these tasks are located in the practice files folder for Microsoft OneNote 2010. You can save the results of these exercises in the same folder. Change the file name so that you don't overwrite the sample files. When you are done, try performing the following tasks:

- Open the notebook Home Improvements.
- Insert a link to the file Estimate.xlsx.
- Insert a link to one of your favorite websites.
- Attach the file Estimate.xlsx.
- Insert a printout of the file Proposal.pptx.
- If you have a scanner, insert a scanned image to this notebook.

4.3 Edit Text in OneNote

The text you add to notes can be formatted and edited by using a variety of tools, many of which appear on the OneNote ribbon's Home tab. You can also make use of commands on the Review tab to conduct research, look up the definitions of words and find their synonyms, check facts and figures from sites on the Internet, and translate passages of text.

You'll learn the details of how you edit and format text and how to work in the Research pane in the topics in this section.

Using the Format Painter

If you have worked with Office applications in recent years, you are most likely familiar with the Format Painter, the tool that lets you copy formatting and apply it to another location. In OneNote 2010 (and other Office 2010 applications), the Format Painter appears in the Clipboard group on the ribbon's Home tab.

To start, select the text or other content that contains the formatting you want to copy and apply to other content. Then, on the Home tab, click the Format Painter and drag the pointer across the text you want to apply the formatting to. If you want to apply the copied formatting to more than one location, double-click the Format Painter button after you select the formatted content you want to copy.

➤ To use the Format Painter

1. Select the text with the formatting you want to copy.
2. On the **Home** tab, click the **Format Painter** button. (Double-click the button if you want to apply the formatting to more than one location.)
3. Drag across the text you want to apply the copied formatting to.

Applying Styles

OneNote comes with 11 built-in styles you can apply to the text in a notebook. You cannot create your own styles or modify the styles that come with OneNote, but the gallery of styles that are available provides six levels of headings, a style for page titles, styles for citations and quotations, a style for programming code, and the Normal style.

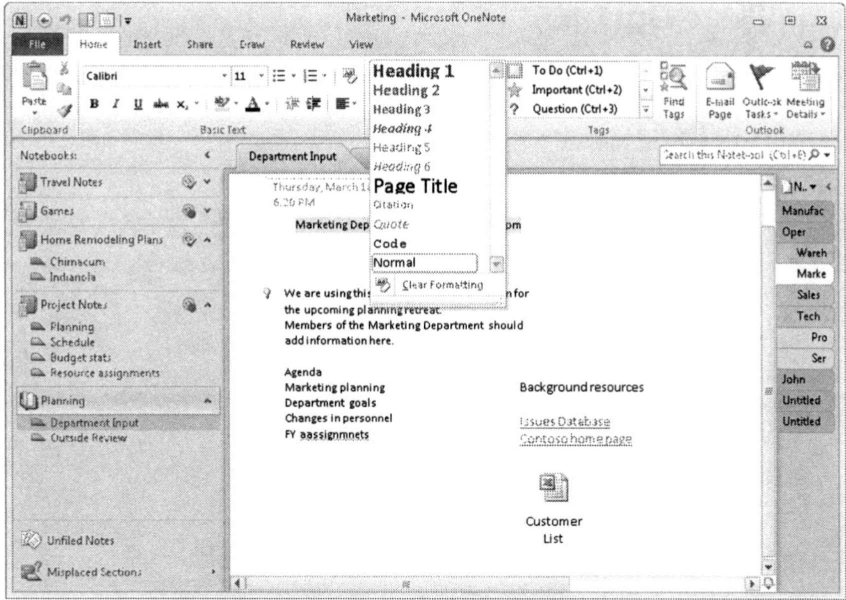

You cannot modify styles or create your own styles in OneNote, but the built-in options provide a useful set of styles for headings and body text.

To apply a style, select the paragraph you want to apply the style to, open the Styles gallery on the Home tab, and then select the style you want to use. OneNote applies a style to all the text in the current paragraph. (No text needs to be selected.)

You can use several keyboard combinations to apply styles. Press Ctrl+Alt+1 through Ctrl+Alt+6 to apply the corresponding heading styles. Press Ctrl+Shift+N to apply the built-in Normal style.

> **Tip** To format the page title, press Ctrl+Shift+T to select the page title and then apply any formatting you prefer in lieu of the Page Title style.

➤ To apply a style

1. Select the paragraph you want to apply the style to.
2. Open the **Styles** gallery on the **Home** tab, and then select the style you want to use.

Using Paste Options

When you copy text to the Windows Clipboard, OneNote provides four options for how you can format the text when you paste it. These options appear in the Paste Options gallery on the Home tab.

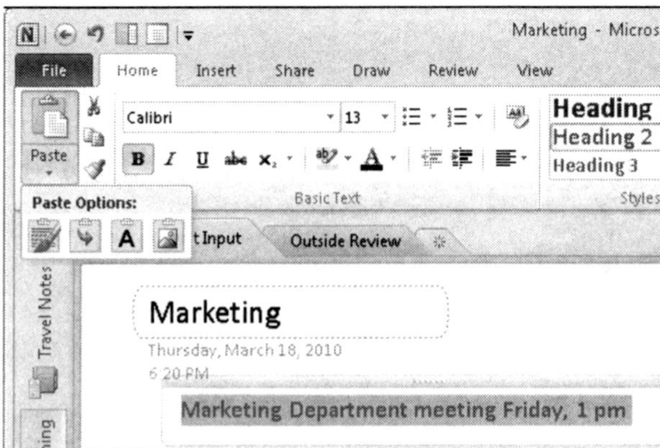

The four paste options let you control how the text you paste is formatted.

The following lists describes the effect each paste option provides:

- **Keep Source Formatting** Choose this option if you want to preserve the formatting that's applied to the text you are pasting. This is the default option, which OneNote applies if you click Paste instead of clicking the down arrow to display the paste options.
- **Merge Formatting** If you choose Merge Formatting and paste the text into an existing note container, the text you paste picks up the formatting applied to the text in the container.
- **Keep Text Only** This option removes any local formatting applied to the text you paste and also removes any graphics you've copied to the Clipboard.
- **Picture** Choosing this option pastes the text as a static image.

➤ To use paste options

1. On the **Home** tab, click the down arrow below the **Paste** button.
2. In the gallery OneNote displays, click the paste option you want to apply.

Clearing Formatting

If you need to remove the formatting that is applied to text in a notebook, select the text and then choose Clear Formatting at the bottom of the Styles gallery. You can also select the text and press Ctrl+Shift+N to remove formatting and apply the Normal style.

➤ To clear formatting

1. Select the text you want to work with.
2. On the **Home** tab, click the **More** button at the bottom right of the **Styles** gallery.
3. Click **Clear Formatting**.

Working with Tables

You can add a table to a OneNote notebook in several ways:

- Click Table on the Insert tab and then drag through the grid to specify the number of columns and rows.
- Click Table, Insert Table (which appears at the bottom of the grid), and then specify the number of columns and rows by using the controls in the Insert Table dialog box.
- Type the text for the table's first entry (this might be a column heading), and then press Tab to create another column. Click Tab again to create a third column (you don't need to enter any text in the previous cell), and press Enter when you want to start the next row.

When you insert a table (or when you select a table), OneNote displays the Table Tools Layout tab, which you can use to select the entire table or specific columns, rows, or cells; insert or delete columns and rows; hide the table's borders; and align the contents of table cells.

> **Tip** You can access the table layout commands also by right-clicking in a table and choosing Table from the shortcut menu.

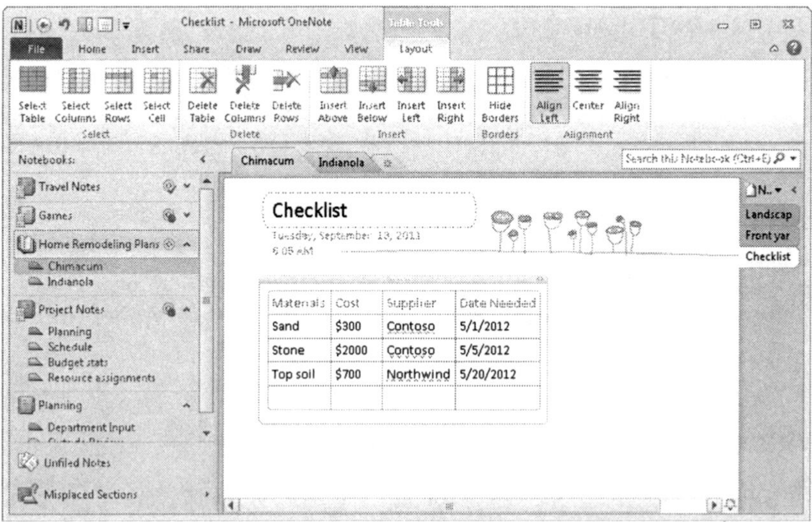

Tables serve many useful purposes in OneNote. Use the Table Tools Layout tab to modify the number of columns and rows and set the alignment of content in the table's cells.

If you like to use keyboard shortcuts, use the following combinations to modify the layout of a table:

- To create a new column to the left or right of the current column, press Ctrl+Alt+E or Ctrl+Alt+R, respectively.
- To create a new row below the current one, even if the insertion point is in the middle of the row, press Ctrl+Enter.
- To create a new row above the current one, move the insertion point to the beginning of the row and press Enter.
- To begin a new paragraph in the same cell, press Alt+Enter.

➤ To insert a table in OneNote

Use one of the following approaches:

- On the **Insert** tab, click **Table**, and then drag through the grid to specify the number of columns and rows.
- On the **Insert** tab, click **Table**, click **Insert Table**, and then specify the number of columns and rows in the **Insert Table** dialog box.
- Type the text for the table's first entry, and then press Tab to create the next column. Press Tab again (with or without entering text first) to create the third column. Press Enter to create the next row.

➤ To change the layout of a table

1. Select the table.
2. On the **Table Tools Layout** tab, use the commands provided to select the table or table elements, insert or delete table elements, hide borders, and align the content of table cells.

Conducting Research

In Chapter 1, you learned about setting options for using the Research pane. In this section, you'll learn more about how to use the Research pane to look up definitions for words you're unfamiliar with, find suitable synonyms by using a thesaurus, and how you can translate the text you select in a notebook.

To open the Research pane and gain access to these features, click the Review tab and then click Research. OneNote displays the Research pane along the right side of the window.

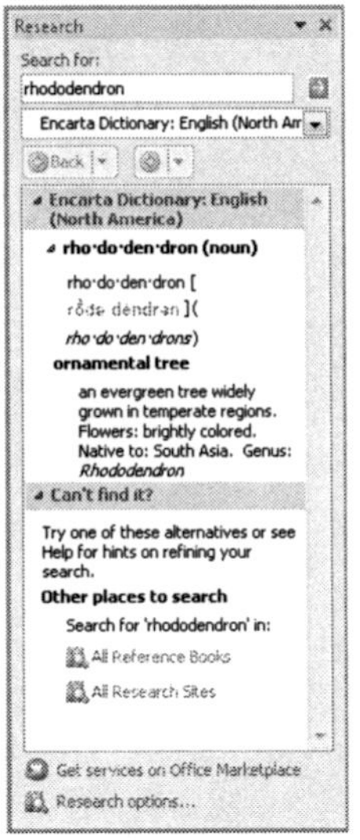

You can use the Research pane for many purposes, including looking up terms in the dictionary, displaying search results from Bing, and translating terms.

Enter the term you want to look up or translate in the Search For box, and then choose the reference source you want to work with. For example, choose Encarta Dictionary to find a definition, or choose Bing to find additional information about a topic or term. You can navigate through recent searches by using the Back (the ScreenTip refers to this button also as Previous Search) and Next Search buttons. The following sections describe several specific operations.

See Also **For details about setting options for working in the Research pane, see "Configuring Research and Translation Options" in Chapter 1.**

Using the Dictionary

To look up the definition of a word, you can use the Encarta Dictionary. Type the term you want to look up in the Search For box, and then choose Encarta Dictionary from the list of references. You can click the phonetic spelling of the word (which appears in a blue font next to the main term) to display a pronunciation guide.

Speakers of English as second language can choose English Assistance from the list of references to obtain definitions as well as usage practices, synonyms, and other information about a term.

Using the Thesaurus

To find a synonym for a term, choose one of the entries for a thesaurus as your reference. (You might see an entry for a thesaurus for more than one language—English, French, and Spanish, for example.) The Research pane lists alternative choices for the term you are looking up. Point to one of the alternatives to display a down arrow you can click to display a menu that lets you insert the term (in place of the one you looked up), copy the term to the Clipboard, or look up the alternative to find additional synonyms.

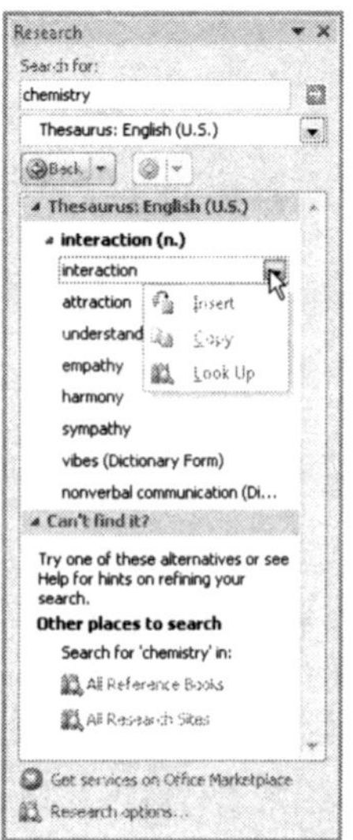

Select a thesaurus from the list of references to find related words. A menu appears when you point to an entry. Choose Insert to add this suggestion to a note.

Translating Text

You can translate a term you enter in the Research pane by choosing Translation from the list of reference sources. The Microsoft Translator shows the term in the language that's selected in the Translation Language Options dialog box.

See Also **For information about working in the Translation Language Options dialog box, see "Configuring Research and Translation Options" in Chapter 1.**

In the Research pane, click Insert to add the translated term at the current insertion point. Click the down arrow beside Insert, and choose Copy to place the translated term on the Clipboard.

You can translate the term into a different language in the Research pane by choosing options in the From and To lists. Depending on the language pairs selected, OneNote uses either the Microsoft Translator or an online dictionary to translate the term. You can see the settings for various language pairs by clicking the Translation Options link in the Research pane to open the Translation Options dialog box.

You can translate a term without first opening the Research pane. Select the term you want to translate, and then click Translate, Translate Selected Text on the OneNote ribbon's Review tab. Choosing this command displays the Research pane with the term translated into the language specified in the Translation Language Options dialog box.

A third approach is to use the mini translator. To enable the mini translator, click Translate, Mini Translator on the Review tab. The text below this command describes how to use the tool, and you'll see the current translation language beside the command's name.

With the mini translator enabled, point to the term you want to translate, and then point to the dimmed image of the mini translator that appears. In the mini translator window, you'll see the translated term plus a set of controls that let you open the Research pane, copy the translated term to the Clipboard, and hear the original term pronounced.

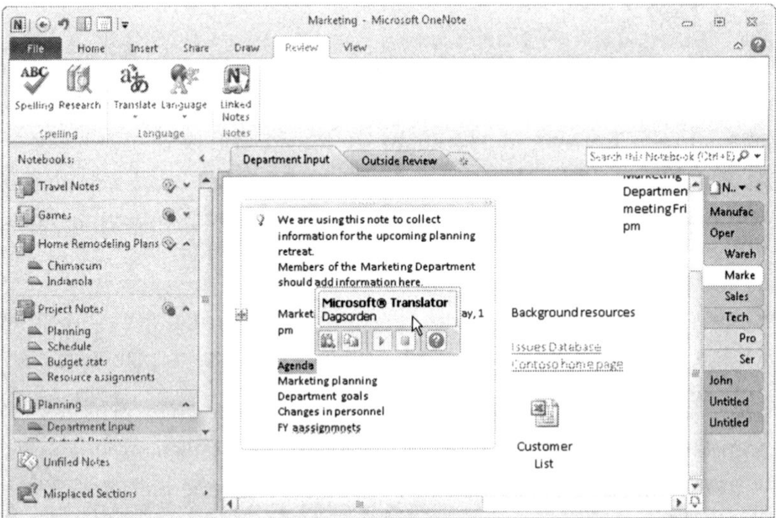

When the mini translator is enabled, you can translate a term by pointing to it.

Practice Tasks

The practice files for these tasks are located in the practice files folder for Microsoft OneNote 2010. You can save the results of these exercises in the same folder. Change the file name so that you don't overwrite the sample files. When you are done, try performing the following tasks:

- Open the notebook Planning Committee.
- Create a simple note as follows:
  - Agenda
  - Welcome
  - Treasurer's report
  - Old Business
  - New Business
- Apply the Heading 2 style to Agenda. Use the tools in the Basic Text group to format the Welcome entry, and then use the Format Painter to apply the formatting to the other items.
- Create another note (you can make up the text), copy the text in this note, and then use the Paste Options to insert the text in the first note.
- Create a table with January, February, and March as column headings, and Revenue, Expense, and Profit as row headings.
- Highlight February in the table, and use the Research pane to translate this text.

4.4 Insert and Modify Visual Elements

To amplify and complement the text and files you add to a OneNote notebook, you can insert pictures and images, create drawings with a pen and shapes, and insert special symbols. In this section, you'll learn the details of how you can work with visual elements in OneNote.

Using Images

The Picture command in the Images group on the Insert tab opens the Insert Picture dialog box. Use this dialog box to select the image file you want to add to a notebook. You can choose from many graphics formats, including .png, .bmp, .jpg, .gif, and others.

After you insert a picture, right-click the image to gain access to commands that let you rotate it, move it behind or in front of other content on the page, move and resize the image, and restore the image to its original size.

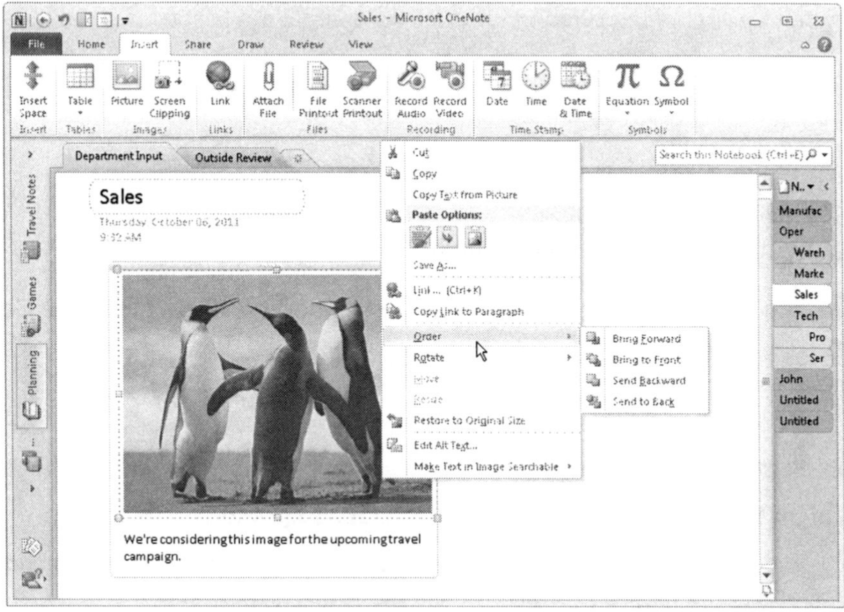

Use this menu to work with pictures you add to a page. The Order command lets you move pictures in front of or behind others.

> **See Also** For details about using an image as a background on a page, see "Setting an Image as a Background" in Chapter 1.

The Edit Alt Text command on the menu opens a dialog box in which you can define the text that a web browser displays as it loads an image or if the image is missing. This text is also used by search engines and to help computer users with disabilities. If the picture you insert contains text (an image of a Microsoft Visio drawing, for example), point to Make Text In Image Searchable and then choose a language, or choose Disable to turn off this feature.

The Screen Clipping command also appears on the Insert tab. Click this command in OneNote, and you'll see that the OneNote window is minimized and the window behind OneNote appears, with the content in that window dimmed. Drag across the window to select the portion of the screen you want to add to the current page. When you release the mouse button, OneNote becomes the active window, and the screen clipping is added.

If OneNote isn't running, press the Windows logo key+S to create a screen clipping. When you release the mouse button, OneNote displays the Select Location In OneNote dialog box, in which you can choose a section or page or use the Copy To Clipboard button to preserve the clipping for use in a separate application.

> **Tip** Screen clippings are tagged with the date and time they are taken. Web pages are also tagged with the page name and the site's URL.

➤ To insert a picture

1. On the **Insert** tab, click **Picture**.
2. In the **Insert Picture** dialog box, open the location where the image file is stored.
3. Select the image, and then click **Insert**.

➤ To add a screen clipping to OneNote

1. Position the window you want to take a clipping from behind OneNote.
2. On the **Insert** tab in OneNote, click **Screen Clipping**.
3. In the window that appears, drag to select the content you want to add, and then release the mouse button.

   The screen clipping is added to the current page.

Inserting Symbols

The Symbols group on the Insert tab contains the Equation command and the Symbol command. The Equation command displays a gallery of standard mathematical expressions (used to calculate the area of a circle, for example, or the Pythagorean Theorem) and the Insert New Equation command, which inserts a placeholder for an equation and displays the Equation Tools Design tab on the OneNote ribbon. This tab lets you select one of the built-in equations or build an equation by inserting symbols and mathematical structures.

The Symbol command shows a small gallery of symbols, including the copyright symbol (©) and the trademark symbol (™) by default. Click More Symbols at the bottom of this gallery to open the Symbol dialog box, in which you can choose accented characters, dingbats, mathematical operators, punctuation marks, and many other types of symbols. Select the character you need, and then click Insert. (You can also double-click the symbol.)

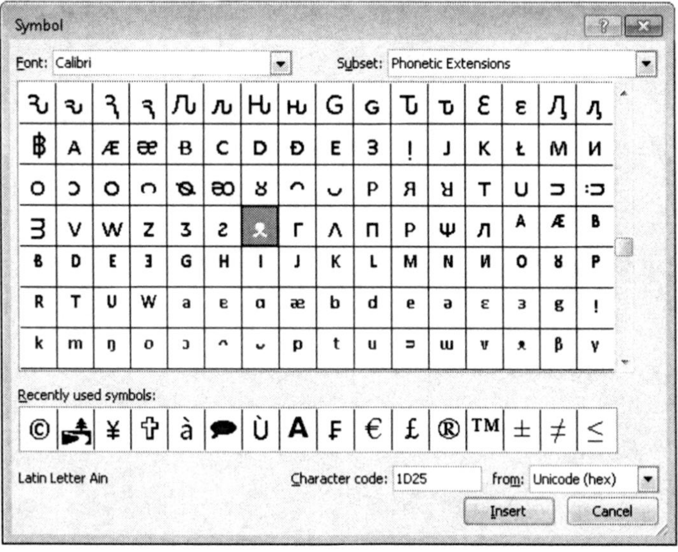

To add a symbol or an accented character, use the Symbol dialog box. Use the Subset list to display specific types of symbols.

Symbols you have inserted recently (or the default set that OneNote shows initially) are grouped at the bottom of the dialog box and in the gallery that OneNote shows when you first click Symbol.

> **Tip** You can enter special symbols by typing the character code shown at the bottom of the Symbol dialog box and then pressing Alt+X.

You can see symbols in a different font by choosing the font you want from the list at the top left of the dialog box. Use the Subset list to see a specific set of symbols—currency symbols, for example, or choices of arrows and fractions.

➤ To insert a symbol

1. On the **Insert** tab, click **Symbol**.
2. Choose a symbol from the gallery, or click **More Symbols** to open the **Symbol** dialog box.
3. Select the font and symbol subset you want to use.
4. Click the symbol, and then click **Insert**.
5. Click **Close** when you finish using the dialog box.

Working with Drawing Tools

To add a sketch, a rough floor plan, or a simple business diagram to a notebook, you work with tools and commands on the Draw tab. The following sections describe the details of working with the commands in each group.

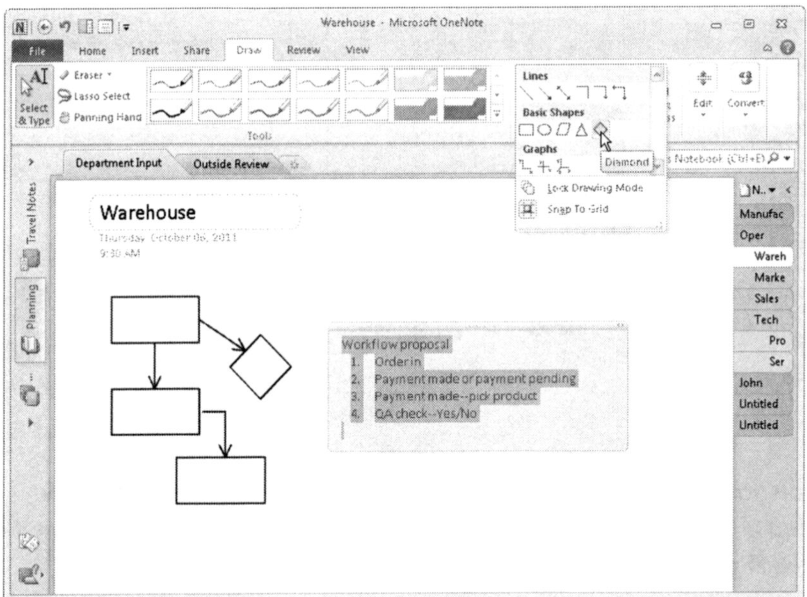

Use the lines, connectors, and basic shapes to create simple business diagrams.

Tools Group

In the Tools group, the Select & Type tool is enabled by default. Use the Eraser tool (you can select an eraser of various sizes) to delete pen strokes and portions of lines and shapes you've added to a page. The Lasso Select tool lets you select irregularly shaped areas of a drawing. The Panning Hand tool lets you scroll a page by using the mouse, a pen, or a finger (for touch-enabled computers).

> **Tip** When you need to type a note again, you don't need to click the Select & Type tool. Just click on the page where you want the note to appear and type; OneNote automatically enables the Select & Type tool again.

> **See Also** You'll learn about working with a pen in the upcoming section "Using and Setting Pen Options."

Insert Shapes Group

The Insert Shapes group provides several line styles (with arrows and without), five basic shapes, and three basic graph patterns. Select a shape (click the More button to reveal the full set of shapes), and then click on the page where you want the shape to appear. The shape is selected when you add it, and you can use the handles on the shape's borders to change the shape's dimensions. You can drag the shape to reposition it.

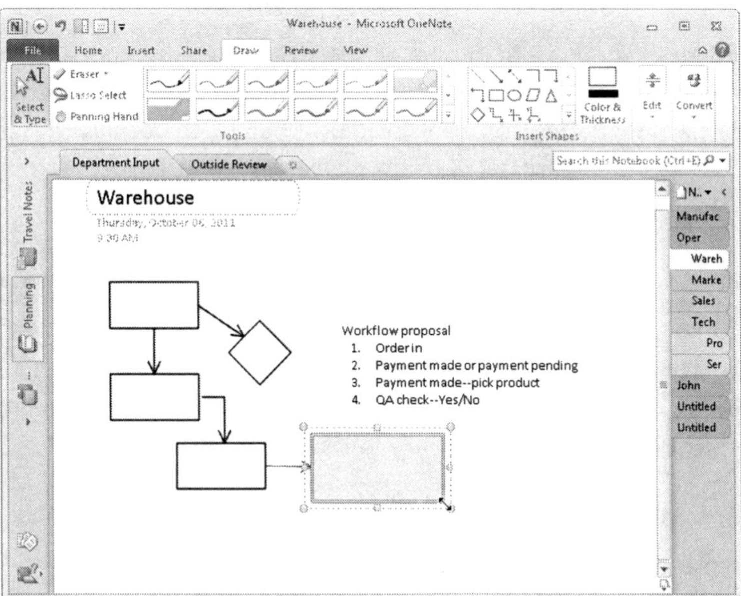

Use the handles on the sides and corners of a shape to resize the shape's dimensions.

> **Tip** When you select a shape, you'll see a mini toolbar that includes a number of the commands on the Draw tab and other commands from OneNote.

If you want to use a different color or a different line thickness for a shape's borders, click Color & Thickness in the Insert Shapes group, and then make the selections you want to use in the Color & Thickness dialog box. The color of the line thickness options changes when you select a line color, which gives you a preview of how the shape borders will appear.

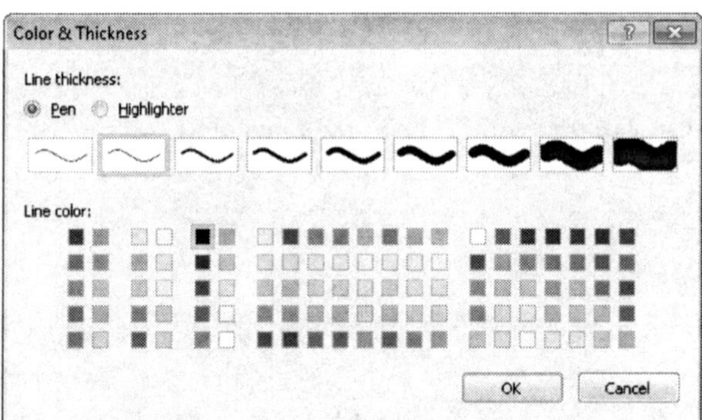

In the Color & Thickness dialog box, you can define the color and thickness for the borders of shapes.

Edit Group

The commands in the Edit group let you do the following:

- **Insert Space** Lets you add or remove space between note containers and other elements on a page. Click the button, and then place the pointer between the two elements whose spacing you want to adjust. Drag up to decrease the space; drag down to add more space between the elements.
- **Delete** Deletes the selected note container or other element.
- **Arrange** Use the options on this menu to position an element behind or in front of other elements.
- **Rotate** When you select an element such as an image or a shape, OneNote enables this command. You can choose an option to rotate the element or to flip the element horizontally or vertically to change its orientation.

Convert Group

The two commands in the Convert group—Ink To Text and Ink To Math—let you convert text and mathematical expressions you initially input by using a pen, for example. The Ink To Text command converts any handwritten notes on the current page to text notes.

When you select Ink To Math, OneNote displays the Insert Ink Equation dialog box. Write the expression or equation you need, and use the dialog box's Preview area to view how OneNote interprets your handwriting. Use the eraser to delete part of an expression. If OneNote misinterprets your handwriting, click Select And Correct, and then drag to select the part of the expression you want OneNote to review. OneNote displays suggested corrections. If you see the correct expression, select it to add it to the Preview area. Note that OneNote doesn't change your handwritten expression, but it is the expression that appears in the Preview area that OneNote will insert in the notebook.

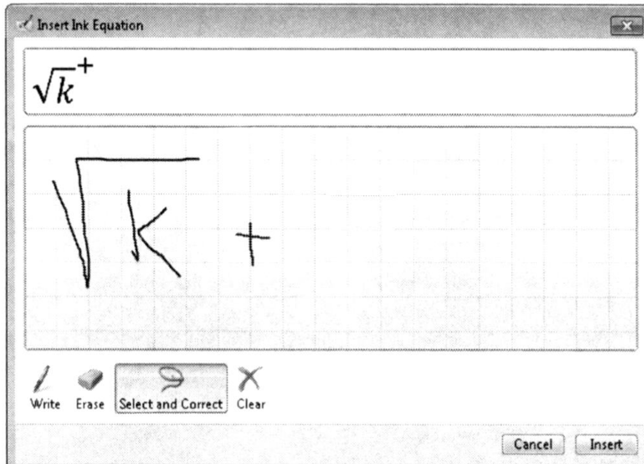

In the Insert Ink Equation dialog box, handwrite an expression and then use the Preview area to see how OneNote interprets your input. You can erase all or portions of what you write or select portions and view suggested corrections.

> **Tip** You can also right-click on a page and point to the Convert command to convert text or mathematical expressions.

➤ To convert ink to text

→ On the **Insert** tab, click **Ink To Text**.

➤ To write and insert mathematical expressions

1. On the **Insert** tab, click **Ink To Math**.
2. In the **Insert Ink Equation** dialog box, write the expression you want to insert.
3. Click the **Erase** button to delete part of the expression.
4. Click the **Select And Correct** button, and drag around a portion of the handwritten expression to see alternative interpretations.
5. Click **Clear** to remove all of the expression.
6. Click **Insert** to add the expression shown in the **Preview** area to the current page.

Using and Setting Pen Options

Included in the Draw tab's Tools group is a large gallery of options for pens and highlighters. Point to an option in the gallery to view a ScreenTip that indicates the color, type (pen or highlighter), and thickness.

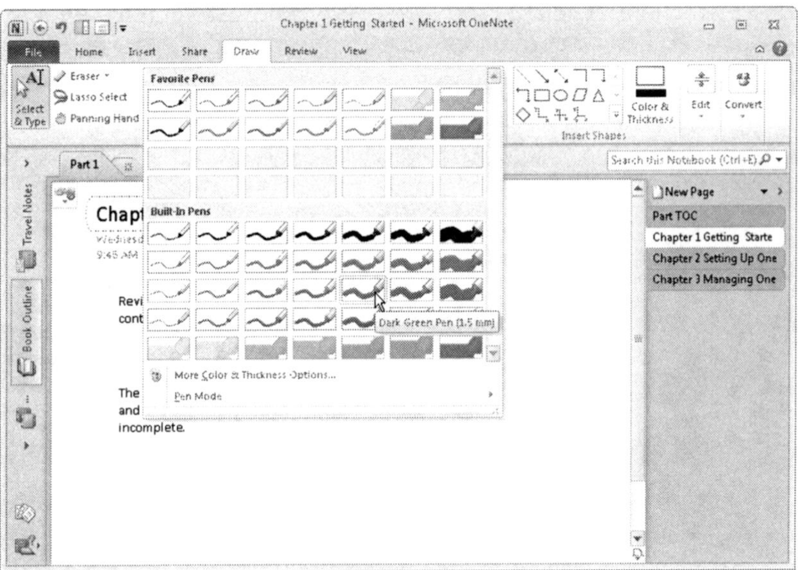

The Pen And Highlighter gallery provides numerous built-in choices.
Click More Color & Thickness Options to define your own.

You can add to the number of pens and highlighters by clicking More Color & Thickness Options at the bottom of the gallery. This command opens the Pen Properties dialog box. In the dialog box, under Stroke Type And Thickness, select Pen or Highlighter and then choose the line thickness you want. Under Line Color, select the color that the pen or highlighter will apply.

The Pen Mode command opens a menu with the following four options:

- **Create Both Handwriting and Drawings** This is the option selected by default. This option lets you convert handwritten notes to text when you add input with a pen.
- **Create Drawings Only** If you choose this option, you disable the Ink To Text command. Handwritten text that you add to a page is represented as a drawing and cannot be converted to text.
- **Create Handwriting Only** Use this option to prevent OneNote from misclassifying your handwriting as a drawing.

- **Use Pen As Pointer** Select this option if you want to use a pen as a pointing device (to select items on page, for example) instead of needing to switch to the Select & Type mode to perform these operations.

Tip **The Advanced page of the OneNote Options dialog box includes three settings for working with pens. These options let you control whether the "scratch out" gesture deletes portions of handwritten notes or drawings, set an option for using pen pressure sensitivity (setting this option increases the file size), and control whether you switch automatically between inking, selecting, typing, and panning.**

Practice Tasks

The practice files for these tasks are located in the practice files folder for Microsoft OneNote 2010. You can save the results of these exercises in the same folder. Change the file name so that you don't overwrite the sample files. When you are done, try performing the following tasks:

- Open the notebook Home Remodeling Plans.
- On a new page in the Garden section, insert one of the sample pictures that comes with Windows.
- In the Symbol dialog box, choose the Calibri font (if it isn't selected) and then choose Dingbats from the Subset list. Insert one or more of these special characters.
- Use the shapes on the Draw tab to create a simple floor plan.
- Create a highlighter that uses the color brown and a 3.0 mm thickness.
- Use the Ink To Math command to create a simple mathematical expression and insert it on a page.

Objective Review

Before finishing this chapter, be sure you have mastered the following skills:

- Use links and linked notes
- Insert files
- Edit text in OneNote
- Insert and modify visual elements

Appendix: OneNote Keyboard Shortcuts

The following tables list the numerous keyboard shortcuts you can use to perform operations in OneNote.

Typing and editing notes

To do this	Press
Open a new OneNote window.	Ctrl+M
Open the side note window.	Ctrl+Shift+M
Dock the OneNote window.	Ctrl+Alt+D
Select all items on the current page.	Ctrl+A
Insert a line break without starting a new paragraph.	Shift+Enter
Check spelling.	F7
Open the thesaurus for the currently selected word.	Shift+F7
Bring up the context menu for any note, tab, or any other object that currently has focus.	Shift+F10
Execute the action suggested on the Information Bar if it appears at the top of a page.	Ctrl+Shift+W

Formatting notes

To do this	Press
Highlight selected text in yellow.	Ctrl+Shift+H or Ctrl+Alt+H
Insert a hyperlink.	Ctrl+K
Copy the formatting of selected text (Format Painter).	Ctrl+Shift+C
Paste the formatting to selected text (Format Painter).	Ctrl+Shift+V
Open a hyperlink. (The cursor must be placed anywhere within the formatted hyperlink text.)	Enter
Apply or remove bold formatting from the selected text.	Ctrl+B
Apply or remove italic formatting from the selected text.	Ctrl+I
Apply or remove the underline from the selected text.	Ctrl+U
Apply or remove strikethrough from the selected text.	Ctrl+Hyphen
Apply or remove superscript formatting from the selected text.	Ctrl+Shift+=

To do this	Press
Apply or remove subscript formatting from the selected text.	Ctrl+=
Apply or remove bulleted list formatting from the selected paragraph.	Ctrl+Period
Apply or remove numbered list formatting from the selected paragraph.	Ctrl+Slash
Apply a Heading 1 style to the current note.	Ctrl+Alt+1
Apply a Heading 2 style to the current note.	Ctrl+Alt+2
Apply a Heading 3 style to the current note.	Ctrl+Alt+3
Apply a Heading 4 style to the current note.	Ctrl+Alt+4
Apply a Heading 5 style to the current note.	Ctrl+Alt+5
Apply a Heading 6 style to the current note.	Ctrl+Alt+6
Apply the Normal style to the current note.	Ctrl+Shift+N
Indent a paragraph from the left.	Alt+Shift+Right Arrow
Remove a paragraph indent from the left.	Alt+Shift+Left Arrow
Right-align the selected paragraph.	Ctrl+R
Left-align the selected paragraph.	Ctrl+L
Increase the font size of selected text.	Ctrl+Shift+>
Decrease the font size of selected text.	Ctrl+Shift+<
Clear all formatting applied to the selected text.	Ctrl+Shift+N
Show or hide rule lines on the current page.	Ctrl+Shift+R

Adding items to a page

To do this	Press
Insert a document or file on the current page.	Alt+N, F
Insert a document or file as a printout on the current page.	Alt+N, O
Show or hide document printouts on the current page (when running OneNote in High Contrast mode).	Alt+Shift+P
Insert a picture from a file.	Alt+N, P
Insert a picture from a scanner or a camera.	Alt+N, S
Insert a screen clipping. (The OneNote icon must be active in the notification area, at the far right of the Windows taskbar.)	Windows logo key+S
Insert the current date.	Alt+Shift+D
Insert the current date and time.	Alt+Shift+F
Insert the current time.	Alt+Shift+T
Insert a line break.	Shift+Enter
Start a math equation or convert selected text to a math equation.	Alt+=
Create a table by adding a second column to already typed text.	Tab
Create another column in a table with a single row.	Tab

To do this	Press
Create another row when at the end cell of a table. (Press Enter a second time to finish the table.)	Enter
Create a row below the current row in a table.	Ctrl+Enter
Create another paragraph in the same cell in a table.	Alt+Enter
Create a column to the right of the current column in a table.	Ctrl+Alt+R
Create a column to the left of the current column in a table.	Ctrl+Alt+E
Create a row above the current one in a table (when the cursor is at the beginning of any row).	Enter
Delete the current empty row in a table (when the cursor is at the beginning of the row).	Press Delete twice

Selecting notes and objects

To do this	Press
Select all items on the current page. (Press Ctrl+A more than once to increase the scope of the selection.)	Ctrl+A
Select to the end of the line.	Shift+End
Select the whole line (when the cursor is at the beginning of the line).	Shift+Down Arrow
Jump to the title of the page and select it.	Ctrl+Shift+T
Cancel the selected outline or page.	Esc
Move the current paragraph or several selected paragraphs up.	Alt+Shift+Up Arrow
Move the current paragraph or several selected paragraphs down.	Alt+Shift+Down Arrow
Move the current paragraph or several selected paragraphs left (decreasing the indent).	Alt+Shift+Left Arrow
Move the current paragraph or several selected paragraphs right (increasing the indent).	Alt+Shift+Right Arrow
Select the current paragraph and its subordinate paragraphs.	Ctrl+Shift+Hyphen
Delete the selected note or object.	Delete
Move to the beginning of the line.	Home
Move to the end of the line.	End
Move one character to the left.	Left Arrow
Move one character to the right.	Right Arrow
Go back to the last page visited.	Alt+Left Arrow
Go forward to the next page visited.	Alt+Right Arrow
Start playback of a selected audio or video recording.	Ctrl+Alt+P
Start playback of a selected audio or video recording.	Ctrl+Alt+S
Rewind the current audio or video recording by a few seconds.	Ctrl+Alt+Y
Fast-forward the current audio or video recording by a few seconds.	Ctrl+Alt+U

Tagging notes*

To do this	Press
Apply, mark, or clear the To Do tag.	Ctrl+1
Apply or clear the Important tag.	Ctrl+2
Apply or clear the Question tag.	Ctrl+3
Apply or clear the Remember for later tag.	Ctrl+4
Apply or clear the Definition tag.	Ctrl+5
Apply or clear the Highlight tag.	Ctrl+6
Apply or clear the Contact tag.	Ctrl+7
Apply or clear the Address tag.	Ctrl+8
Apply or clear the Phone Number tag.	Ctrl+9
Remove all note tags from the selected notes.	Ctrl+0

* This table shows the default shortcuts for applying tags. The shortcuts can be assigned to other tags by customizing tag settings.

Using outlines

To do this	Press
Show through Level 1.	Alt+Shift+1
Expand to Level 2.	Alt+Shift+2
Expand to Level 3.	Alt+Shift+3
Expand to Level 4.	Alt+Shift+4
Expand to Level 5.	Alt+Shift+5
Expand to Level 6.	Alt+Shift+6
Expand to Level 7.	Alt+Shift+7
Expand to Level 8.	Alt+Shift+8
Expand to Level 9.	Alt+Shift+9
Expand all levels.	Alt+Shift+0
Increase indent by one level.	Tab
Decrease indent by one level.	Shift+Tab
Expand a collapsed outline.	Alt+Shift+plus sign
Collapse an expanded outline.	Alt+Shift+minus sign

Working with pages and side notes

To do this	Press
Enable or disable full page view.	F11
Expand or collapse the tabs of a page group.	Ctrl+Shift+*
Print the current page.	Ctrl+P
Add a new page at the end of the selected section.	Ctrl+N

To do this	Press
Increase the width of the page tabs bar.	Ctrl+Shift+[
Decrease the width of the page tabs bar.	Ctrl+Shift+]
Create a new page below the current page tab at the same level.	Ctrl+Alt+N
Decrease indent level of the current page tab label.	Ctrl+Alt+[
Increase indent level of the current page tab label.	Ctrl+Alt+]
Create a new subpage below the current page.	Ctrl+Shift+Alt+N
Select the current page.	Ctrl+Shift+A If the selected page is part of a group, press Ctrl+A to select all of the pages in the group.
Go to the first page in the currently visible set of page tabs.	Alt+Page Up
Go to the last page in the currently visible set of page tabs.	Alt+Page Down
Scroll up in the current page.	Page Up
Scroll down in the current page.	Page Down
Scroll to the top of the current page.	Ctrl+Home
Scroll to the bottom of the current page.	Ctrl+End
Go to the next paragraph.	Ctrl+Down Arrow
Go to the previous paragraph.	Ctrl+Up Arrow
Move the insertion point up in the current page, or expand the page up.	Ctrl+Alt+Up Arrow
Move the insertion point down in the current page, or expand the page down.	Ctrl+Alt+Down Arrow
Move the insertion point left in the current page, or expand the page to the left.	Ctrl+Alt+Left Arrow
Move the insertion point right in the current page, or expand the page to the right.	Ctrl+Alt+Right Arrow
Go to the next note container.	Alt+Down Arrow
Go back to the last page visited.	Alt+Left Arrow
Go forward to the next page visited.	Alt+Right Arrow
Zoom in.	Alt+Ctrl+plus sign (on the numeric keypad) –or– Alt+Ctrl+Shift+plus sign
Zoom out.	Alt+Ctrl+minus sign (on the numeric keypad) –or– Alt+Ctrl+Shift+Hyphen
Save changes. (While OneNote is running, your notes are automatically saved whenever you change them. Manually saving notes is not necessary.)	Ctrl+S

Working with notebooks and sections

To do this	Press
Create a new section.	Ctrl+T
Open a notebook.	Ctrl+O
Open a section.	Ctrl+Alt+Shift+O
Go to the next section.	Ctrl+Tab
Go to the previous section.	Ctrl+Shift+Tab
Go to the next page in the section.	Ctrl+Page Down
Go to the previous page in the section.	Ctrl+Page Up
Go to the first page in the section.	Alt+Home
Go to the last page in the section.	Alt+End
Go to the first page in the currently visible set of page tabs.	Alt+Page Up
Go to the last page of the currently visible set of page tabs.	Alt+Page Down
Move or copy the current page.	Ctrl+Alt+M
Put focus on the current page tab.	Ctrl+Alt+G
Select the current page tab.	Ctrl+Shift+A
Put focus on the current section tab.	Ctrl+Shift+G
Move the current section.	Shift+F10, M
Switch to a different notebook on the Navigation bar.	Ctrl+G, then press Down Arrow or Up Arrow keys to select a different notebook, and then press Enter

Searching notes

To do this	Press
Move the insertion point to the search box to search all notebooks.	Ctrl+E
While searching all notebooks, preview the next result.	Down Arrow
While searching all notebooks, go to the selected result and dismiss Search.	Enter
Change the search scope.	Ctrl+E, Tab, Space
Open the Search Results pane.	Alt+O after searching
Search only the current page. (You can switch between searching everywhere and searching only the current page at any point by pressing Ctrl+E or Ctrl+F.	Ctrl+F
While searching the current page, move to the next result.	Enter or F3
While searching the current page, move to the previous result.	Shift+F3
Dismiss Search and return to the page.	Esc

Sharing notes

To do this	Press
Send the selected pages in an e-mail message.	Ctrl+Shift+E
Create a Today Outlook task from the currently selected note.	Ctrl+Shift+1
Create a Tomorrow Outlook task from the currently selected note.	Ctrl+Shift+2
Create a This Week Outlook task from the currently selected note.	Ctrl+Shift+3
Create a Next Week Outlook task from the currently selected note.	Ctrl+Shift+4
Create a No Date Outlook task from the currently selected note.	Ctrl+Shift+5
Open the selected Outlook task.	Ctrl+Shift+K
Mark the selected Outlook task as complete.	Ctrl+Shift+9
Delete the selected Outlook task.	Ctrl+Shift+0
Sync changes in the current shared notebook.	Shift+F9
Sync changes in all shared notebooks.	F9
Mark the current page as unread.	Ctrl+Q

Password-protecting sections

To do this	Press
Lock all password-protected sections.	Ctrl+Alt+L

Index

Symbols

A

B

C

D

E

F

H

I

K

L

M

Q

R

S

About the Author

John Pierce worked as an editor and writer at Microsoft Corporation for 12 years and is the author or coauthor of *MOS 2010 Study Guide for Microsoft Word Expert, Excel Expert, Access, and SharePoint*; *Microsoft Access 2003 Inside Track*, *Microsoft Office Groove 2007 Step by Step*, *Microsoft Small Business Kit*, and other books. He is now a freelance editor and writer who frequently works on books and articles related to Microsoft software and technologies.

What do you think of this book?

We want to hear from you!

To participate in a brief online survey, please visit:

microsoft.com/learning/booksurvey

Tell us how well this book meets your needs—what works effectively, and what we can do better. Your feedback will help us continually improve our books and learning resources for you.

Thank you in advance for your input!

CPSIA information can be obtained at www.ICGtesting.com
Printed in the USA
LVOW120457120612

285718LV00001B/3/P

9 780735 665941